AMERICAN CONTRADICTIONS

AMERICAN CONTRADICTIONS

Interviews with Nine American Writers

Edited by

Wolfgang Binder and

Helmbrecht Breinig

Wesleyan University Press
Published by
University Press of New England
Hanover and London

Wesleyan University Press
Published by University Press of New England, Hanover, NH 03755

The interviews contained in this volume were originally published in German, together with a selection of literary texts, as *Facing America: Multikulturelle Literatur der heutigen U.S.A. in Texten und Interviews: Ein Lesebuch* by Rotpunktverlag Zurich, 1994.

Printed in the United States of America 5 4 3 2 1
CIP data appear at the end of the book

All photographs are by Bernd Böhner except for the photograph of Ishmael Reed, which is by Harald Zapf.

CONTENTS

Introduction vii
by Helmbrecht Breinig and Wolfgang Binder

1. *ROBERTO G. FERNÁNDEZ* 1
interviewed by Wolfgang Binder

2. *ANDREW HOLLERAN* 19
interviewed by Christina Strobel

3. *ALAN LELCHUK* 49
interviewed by Regine Rosenthal

4. *GRACE PALEY* 77
interviewed by Birgit Fromkorth and Susanne Opfermann

5. *ISHMAEL REED* 101
interviewed by Wolfgang Binder and Harald Zapf

6. *LUCI TAPAHONSO* 111
interviewed by Helmbrecht Breinig and Klaus Lösch

7. *ED VEGA* 125
interviewed by Wolfgang Binder

8. *GERALD VIZENOR* 143
interviewed by Helmbrecht Breinig and Klaus Lösch

9. *JOHN A. WILLIAMS* 167
interviewed by Wolfgang Binder

Selected Bibliography 185

INTRODUCTION

Helmbrecht Breinig and Wolfgang Binder

In 1751, Benjamin Franklin commented upon the influx of German immigrants into Pennsylvania:

> And since Detachments of English from Britain sent to America, will have their Places at Home so soon supply'd and increase so largely here; why should the Palatine Boors be suffered to swarm into our Settlements, and by herding together establish their Language and Manners, to the Exclusion of ours? Why should Pennsylvania, founded by the English, become a Colony of *Aliens,* who will shortly be so numerous as to Germanize us instead of our Anglifying them, and will never adopt our Language or Customs, any more than they can acquire our Complexion.[1]

It seems somewhat ironic that the descendants of German immigrants indeed form one of the most numerous sections of the American population yet also belong to one of the most completely assimilated and hence invisible, inaudible, and almost unnoticeable ethnic groups. There is more irony in the observation that Franklin gives an early instance of nativist argumentation—animal imagery and all—such as might be heard today almost verbatim both in the United States and in Germany, the Palatine Boors having been replaced by, say, Mexicans or Turks. While American citizens tend to suppress their knowledge of the extent of multiculturality in their country, Europeans will ignore the fact that even their nation-states have never been as monocultural as chauvinist discourse has it.

The clash of such discourse (often enhanced by racism and religious fanaticism) with multicultural social reality may lead to "ethnic purifications"—witness of this being the Holocaust and, in our own day, Bosnia. It is with such a past and such a present in mind that one branch of European intellectuals turns to the United States as an example of the supposedly peaceful concourse of cultures. The prominent role of the American women's liberation movement and the recognition that gays and lesbians have achieved in some parts of the country seem to confirm the model character of America even beyond the confines of ethnicity. For such enthusiasts, American exceptionalism is not just a historical claim and a promise but a solid fact. In a recent book review in the influential German newsmagazine *Der Spiegel,* Maxim Biller wholeheartedly adopts exceptionalist arguments as they have been expressed almost since the American Revolution:

> Is America really better off? But of course. For to this day no Reagan, McCarthy and Nixon, no redneck and WASP racist, no CIA-supported Central American dictator and transatlantic Christian Democratic friend of America has ever managed to do away with the dynamics and the revolutionary civic power of the Bill of Rights.
>
> Why is this so? Because the United States continues to be a—fortunately very powerful—country where the national allegiance of the individual is determined neither ethnically nor culturally nor territorially but solely on the basis of a political agreement: You become American by voluntary decision—as an immigrant you have opted for democracy, for pluralism and equality, for difference and solidarity. That this agreement is violated over and over again does not annihilate it but, on the contrary, continues to keep it alive. And that's what we call the self-purifying effect of civilization.
>
> No American would ever ask who he is and how he is—but only what he wants.[2]

While such optimism may have become rare after the TV pictures of burning city blocks in South Central Los Angeles, American cultural life, at least, is often seen as coherent albeit pluralistic. When literature addresses social issues, it is frequently perceived by Europeans as being a matter of class much more so than of ethnicity or even race, and the articulation of gender interests counts as one among many competing political factors contributing to the play of democracy. Whether their image of

America is positive or negative, Europeans tend to accept the special status of America as a given.

It was with the intention of correcting such simplifying notions that the editors invited a group of American writers from a plurality of cultural backgrounds to discuss their views on multiculturalism, on their own concepts of personal and cultural identity, on their art and on the role that writers play or ought to play in society at large or in their respective groups, on the emancipation processes at home and abroad, and thus on postcolonialism, which now, half a millennium after the age of the so-called discoveries, has become an international cultural phenomenon. That this meeting took place in the university town of Erlangen served another purpose besides enlightening the German audience, namely, that of offering the writers a kind of neutral territory where they might leave behind their usual literary circles as well as the precincts of their cultural groups and, at the same time, gain a vantage point from which to view and comment upon the developments at home. Needless to say, the usual obstacles—finances and previous commitments—prevented the presence of writers from some other groups. Since our aim was to present pluralism and at the same time openness, not only of the national culture but also of any group concept, we considered the gaps in the cross section of multicultural American literature of today as of minor importance.

The authors were invited because of the quality of their literary work and the variety of aesthetic concepts displayed by their writings. They were also invited as representatives of certain groups defined by ethnicity, gender, and sexual preference—the criteria usually applied when we talk about multiculturality and multiculturalism. But just as each writer insisted on the individuality of her or his creative vision, though none of them denied having to perform a function in and for society, each of them also personified a specific combination of group and other allegiances that make the usual concepts of cultural plurality look like rather crude instruments of categorization.

Thus, Gerald Vizenor, one of the leading Native American

fiction writers, and an outstanding poet, essayist, critic, and Berkeley professor of ethnic studies, is of mixed Chippewa and European descent. Although he is an ardent advocate of urban and reservation Indian rights, he emphasizes what he calls his "crossblood" heritage and propagates the cultural mix as a kind of natural condition of contemporary humanity. Just as his postmodern novels combine elements of contemporary experimental fiction as well as of oral traditions and of a variety of other sources, they also present social and cultural groups as being fluid and identities as being the result of choice, chance, and discursive construction rather than as being racially or ethnically determined. He favors transformation and liberation from all kinds of dominance in place of essentialism and the rigidity of scientific classification. Therefore, he see Native American literature in a line with international postcolonialism rather than with some kind of mainstream American culture. His notion of tribalism is thus a far cry from any static and racially or ethnographically defined image of what it means to be an American Indian today. The Navajo poet Luci Tapahonso, on the other hand, belongs to a younger generation, and although she also teaches at an American university, she is firmly rooted in the world she has come from: her clan, her family, her region on the reservation. Her bilingual texts are informed by the rich oral poetic and narrative tradition of her people. For her, "the culture that we come from matters," because in her case it is largely intact, in spite of all the inroads of the modern world and the dominant civilization, but she is aware of her exceptionality in this respect. To group her together with Vizenor reveals the tenuousness of the label "American Indian" for a discrete ethnic group, although she shares with others the burden and the opportunity of dealing with the conflict of languages and literary traditions.

Gender roles are of the essence in matriarchal Navajo society, but for this very reason feminism is out of place there. Quite the opposite is the case in the world of Grace Paley, who, as a youthful septuagenarian, refutes any categorization by generation. Her brilliant, often wonderfully ironic short stories have made her an outstanding exponent of Jewish writing in America, and yet she denies belonging to a group called "Jewish-American writers." While the life she depicts is undoubtedly American and while many of her characters show signs of their Jewish background, other and much less ethno- or nation-specific aspects are considerably more important: generational conflicts, marital relations, the search for values in ordinary, seemingly banal lives. Paley, essayist and spokesperson standing up for human rights, ecological issues, and above all, for feminism, finds her identity less in her ethnic background than in her gender and her political responsibility. By way of contrast, Alan Lelchuk, like Paley also of Russian Jewish extraction, belongs to a younger group of writers but has no problems with being identified with Jewish-American culture and literature as they are represented by figures like Saul Bellow, Philip Rahv, or Philip Roth. And yet his existence as a professor at an Ivy League college and his fascination with the American sports culture add facets to his cultural identity making simple groupings look suspect.

Similar problems apply to the cultural placing of other writers as well. Andrew Holleran is internationally known as one of the first exponents of a distinct gay literature in the United States, and his recent texts form a deeply moving requiem for gay culture in the period of AIDS. The only Anglo-American among the authors invited, he thus simultaneously represents the dominant and one of the most marginalized groups. One may wonder, though, whether his fascination with New York City life doesn't create equally strong ties to other literary representatives of New York culture, for instance, Grace Paley and the Puerto Rican–American writer Ed Vega. His identification with a dying culture, on the other hand, links him to the bilingual Cuban-American novelist Roberto Fernández, whose humorous and satiric portrayals of Cuban exiles of white upper-middle-class descent in Miami set his work apart from other Latino literature in the United States. Fernández rejects the label *Hispanic* as one ignoring national but also ethnic aspects. For the Puerto Rican Ed Vega, who writes in English, the comprehensive term *Hispanic* is also a misnomer, but he equally objects to being categorized as an American. His notion of a Puerto Rican identity is not restricted to a certain ethnicity, as is that of Fernández's group of Cubans, but is defined by a national culture. John A. Williams, one of the most prominent writers of African-American literature, has done much to reduce stereotypical images of black American culture and to develop a kind of historical novel writing suited to the experiences of this part of the population. Ishmael Reed, on the other hand, is a much more radical spokesman for African-American rights. A satirist like Fernández, an experimental writer like Vizenor, he too is part of an international postcolonial and at the same time postmodern movement against all sorts of racial, national, and social dominance as well as against the hegemony of cultural mainstreams and the privileging of certain literary forms. His own syncretism is strongly influenced by the interplay of a plurality of black cultural traditions in Haiti and thus, again, calls into question the notion of homogeneous ethnic groups.

Of those invited to Erlangen, Reed was the most ardent advocate of multiculturalism—for him, monoculturalism amounts to totalitarianism. Yet in his case it also becomes obvious that multiculturalism does not result in the orchestral polyphonic harmony that Horace M. Kallen envisioned in his *Cultural Pluralism* as early as 1924 but will lead to a competition of cultural groups. Reed does not hesitate to point an accusing finger at feminists for what he sees as a quasi-fascist monopolizing of public opinion or at Latinos, Jews, and Asian-Americans for their role in recent ethnic quarrels in several American cities. His option for the African-American part of his family heritage over his Irish and Native American ancestors raises some questions: Can cultural identity be a matter of choice? And to what extent are people prelabeled by the visibility or invisibility of their group affiliation?

Multiculturalism, then, became one of the focal points of the round-table discussion at Erlangen as well as of the interviews. While multiculturality is an old and universal phenomenon, the New Immigration, the tendency toward bilingualism in parts of

America, the expected shift to nonwhite majorities in some of the states—and also the migrations between the countries of Europe and the influx of people from so-called underdeveloped countries—have given the question of how to deal with these changes in education and other cultural institutions an overwhelming urgency on both sides of the Atlantic.

Most of the authors are mildly critical of the commercialization of multiculturalism by the media and by textbook publishers, of its being made a commodity, and of the activism of what Vizenor called the "multiculture cultists," but all of them prefer it to a return to a dominant culture and tradition. Still, questions such as those John Higham has raised, explicitly or implicitly, in a recent article bother not just university teachers but also literary writers: Is multiculturalism a way to more or to less equality? Should group loyalty be strengthened or rather subdued because it may lead to internecine conflicts? Should autonomy and separateness of the individual groups be furthered or reduced? Should multiculturalist activities tend toward conservation of cultural traditions or result in the creation of new and revolutionary concepts?[3]

In his introduction to the MLA forum, "Multiculturalism: The Task of Literary Representation in the Twenty-First Century," Houston A. Baker somewhat loftily declares: "During the past quarter century . . . we who have been othered have awakened."[4] But the first contributor, Henry Louis Gates, Jr., points out that if multiculturalism is about the representation of difference, we need to ask which differences and whose differences. If the answer is the differences of cultural identities, then we have to admit that gender identity, sexual identity, racial identity, while always "socially inflected and produced, rather than unmediatedly natural,"[5] simply do not belong to the same category. Gates goes on to show that the comprehensive use of the term "ethnicity" not only camouflages such categorial difficulties but also the difference between dominant and subordinate cultures and that it often serves as a euphemism for "race." As the example of the authors in this volume reveals, even the differentiation demanded by Gates will not suffice, because the intricate network of individual and, on various levels, group allegiances makes the interplay of cultural and personal identity a tricky issue.

In the context of literature an emphasis on a simplified concept of ethnicity courts the additional danger of ignoring the uniqueness of an author's voice and of reducing the question of authenticity to the representation of ethnically relevant material—"under the sign of multiculturalism, literary readings are often guided by the desire to elicit, first and foremost, indices of ethnic particularity, especially those that can be construed as oppositional, transgressive, subversive."[6] It is not surprising, then, that the authors balk at being trammeled by facile multiculturalist labeling even while they support the liberating aspects of the movement. What emerges in the interviews collected in this volume is not so much a collection of statements reflecting just one ethnic or other affiliation but a series of reflections on the entanglement of personal and collective roots, on poetics (of which the authors represent a wide variety), on the aims of artistic expression and political engagement, on the publishing industry, and on the cultural situation for the individual, group, nation, and world. Again and again the statements transcend the situation in the United States and address global issues. While multiculturalism seemingly supports a tendency toward the fragmentation of national cultures, it also reveals that literary aims and formal developments are increasingly shared by an international community of writers, a tendency working as a counterforce to a solipsistic fixation on group traditions and group demands. There are quite a few similarities between the debates on multiculturalism going on in Britain and the United States, other European countries following suit. The plurilocal affiliations of, notably, Caribbean writers but also of authors from India and Pakistan or various parts of Africa with more or less temporary residence in Britain, Canada, and the United States have contributed to an internationalization of multicultural tendencies, and the same can be said of French-speaking writers. The literature of political, social, or sexual liberation has produced an international exchange of traditions as well as of forms of escape from such traditions. Significantly, quite a few of the authors present in Erlangen reacted to questions concerning the Columbus quincentennial by insisting that the time of merely feeling victimized was over, that this was indeed the postcolonial period, and that the moment had come for a less defensive and more future-oriented attitude with respect to self and other.

The fact that most of the writers had not known each other and often not even each other's writings before the conference started attests to the immensity of the American literary scene and the vast number of people involved but also to the compartmentalization of American culture. On the other hand, the ease with which friendships were formed across the borderlines of ethnicity, age, or gender once again gave evidence of the permeability of cultural groups. For some, such openness furnished proof that an all-American culture and society exists, after all, while others regarded it more in terms of a global community.

The exchange of opinions across the cultural boundaries as well as between Americans and Europeans was felt to be so rewarding that the authors themselves suggested publishing the interviews taped during the conference, not only in German translation but also in the original version for the benefit of American readers. These interviews appear here in the alphabetical order of the writers' names, as to group them according to cultural affiliation would have belied the very plurality of allegiances their statements bear witness to.

As was to be expected, the authors handled the interviews quite individually—some answering reluctantly, others volubly; some speaking in an improvised, everyday manner and others in a complex and literary language. Their styles might resemble that of their literary writings or be as removed from it as, for instance, Grace Paley's colloquialisms are from the laconic wit and verbal brilliance of her short stories. Where Vizenor's interview turns into a series of cultural essays, Reed confines himself to some terse political statements. Thus, even in the context of a literary event focusing on certain dominant topics, the interviews reveal much not only about literary concepts or cultural and political opinions but also about personal traits. We have not tried to reduce such diversity by extensive editing but rather consider it a significant feature of the book.

NOTES

1. "Observations concerning the Increase of Mankind, Peopling of Countries, &c.," *The Papers of Benjamin Franklin,* vol. 4, ed. L. W. Labaree et al. (New Haven, Conn.: Yale University Press), p. 234.

2. *Der Spiegel,* January 17, 1994, p. 158; our translation.

3. "Multiculturalism and Universalism: A History and Critique," *American Quarterly* 45 (June 1993): 195–219. Cf. also the rejoinders by Gerald Early, Gary Gerstle, Nancy A. Hewitt, and Vicki L. Ruiz in the same issue.

4. *Profession 93* (New York: MLA, 1993), p. 5.

5. "Beyond the Culture Wars: Identities in Dialogue," *Profession 93* (New York: MLA, 1993), p. 6.

6. Ibid., p. 8.

AMERICAN CONTRADICTIONS

ONE

ROBERTO G. FERNÁNDEZ

interviewed by Wolfgang Binder

Roberto G. Fernández was born in Sagua la Grande, Cuba, in 1951 and came with his family to the United States in 1961 after the Bay of Pigs fiasco. He belongs to the Cuban-American writers who were educated in the United States and publish in both Spanish and English. Today he is a professor of Latin American and Hispanic literatures at the State University of Florida in Tallahassee, where he received his doctorate in 1978.

His first two books were short story collections published in Spanish: Cuentos sin rumbo *(1975) and* El jardín de la luna *(1976). His most frequent literary subject is the Cuban presence in Florida, especially in the Miami area. Roberto Fernández deals with this material not only with nostalgia but with humor and satire. In* La vida es un special *(1981) and in his most successful novel to date,* Raining Backwards *(1988), he uses the traditions of Cuba before Castro as they are preserved on the mainland, where they often appear moving, chaotic, or grotesque.*

WB: Roberto, when were you born and where?

RF: I was born on September 24, 1951, in Havana. But officially, my papers say I was born in Sagua la Grande because my father didn't want to take the trouble to drive to Havana every time to get some legal documents, so he falsified my papers.

WB: How many children were there?

RF: Just myself and my brother. Two.

WB: And what occupation did your father have?

RF: My father started to be an accountant, and he managed my grandfather's businesses.

WB: He had several businesses?

RF: Yes, he did.

WB: In which areas?

RF: He had an insurance company. They had two sugar mills. I don't like to talk about all those things because those are the things many Cubans in the U.S. will tell you, and it's not true.

WB: Oh, I know. It's your background. Please do.

RF: And there was also an import/export company.

WB: So you were well-to-do?

RF: Oh yes. My family had ten thousand acres of land. Oh my God! I'm sounding just like them!

WB: Did everybody in your family leave Cuba in '59 or '61?

RF: All of my father's side left Cuba. Some of my mother's side stayed.

WB: So at what age did you come to the United States?

RF: I was ten.

WB: And where did your parents settle down?

RF: We lived a month in Miami, and then we settled in Vero Beach. We stayed there for a year. My father went to work for a sugar mill. And after that we moved to Belle Glade, in 1962 I think it was. And there he worked in the stockroom of the sugar mill, dispensing nuts and bolts.

WB: So for him it was quite a difficult start because he was not in a leadership position.

RF: Yes, it was a very difficult start for the first year. My mother did not unpack for a year or two. We used to get our clothing from our suitcases.

WB: Did she expect to go back with you?

RF: Oh yes! She thought we were going back to Cuba again. We came on the third of July in 1961.

WB: How could she be so full of illusions?

RF: I don't know. She thought we were going back in February 1962, so I thought I was going back in February 1962. So we ended up living in Belle Glade for ten years. The months became years, and years decades and decades. [*Laughs.*]

WB: When do you think your parents, especially your mother, realized that they might not be able to go back at all? Or didn't they?

RF: Probably in 1970. Since time was passing . . . Her first job was as a maid. And, of course, my mother didn't know anything about being a maid. She was an especially poor cook—we ate a lot of burned food for many years. So she lasted about a month in that job. Then she went to work for a year or so in a packing house. Radishes. And it was fine because all the Cuban bourgeoisie was there, and they would work, picking the radishes from the conveyor belt, and their hands would burn because of the Clorox. But they would work with all their jewelry and their bracelets on. They worked next to the rednecks and other people but always with a sense of class.

WB: Class and pride. So after this, where did you stay?

RF: We stayed in Belle Glade for about ten years. And then my father went to work for the Gulf and Western Company—the one that had Paramount Studios and all that. And then he became the overseas controller for the company. That was a very big jump then. He had gotten used to the American system. And then they moved to New York. Actually, they lived in a town called Montclair in New Jersey. But by that time I was ready to go to junior college.

WB: Where did you go?

RF: I went to Palm Beach Junior College. And then I went to Florida Atlantic University. And then I went to Florida State.

WB: But your parents stayed up north?

RF: They lived up north for three years and then came down to West Palm Beach because he was transferred back to West Palm Beach.

WB: And which field did you major in?

RF: I started in biology. Of course, I couldn't take organic chemistry—good-bye biology. Then I started with linguistics, and I got a master's in linguistics. I got a Ph.D. in literature. At Florida State University I teach mostly Latin American literature and courses in the contemporary novel and Hispanic literature of the U.S.

WB: If somebody asked you for a self-definition, what are you—what kind of nationality, what kind of allegiances do you have?

RF: I am a citizen of Miami!

WB: [*Laughs.*] Why?

RF: Because I'm going to be there with people who have the same experience, who can switch languages, you know, and can talk about things which were so bad when we came over and all those shared experiences that make a people.

WB: So Miami as a territory is very important for you?

RF: Yes. Both emotionally and literarily. Especially since I live in exile in Tallahassee. [*Both laugh.*] Which is good, because it gave, and it gives me, a different perspective of Miami.

WB: We'll get back to that later. One of the terms that during this conference in Erlangen—and as you know, in the press and the media on both sides of the Atlantic—has been played up a lot is *multiculturalism*. How do you feel about this as a definition for American contemporary society?

RF: Well, it is a multicultural society, but people don't know that it is a multicultural society, and they resist it.

WB: Who resists?

RF: The establishment.

WB: Really?

RF: Yes. Sometimes they pay lip-service to it. And sometimes they have to do it because there is no other option. For instance, in the English Department there is a faction that refuses to teach anything but Anglo-American or English or the European tradition but none of the literatures from other places. I think it betrays what the United States is all about. Because it's just presenting one side. The culture is multi, of course; you have many faces. When you don't present it to the students, the other people think their cultural experience has no value. I mean, you shouldn't just present what you call the ethnic writers because they are ethnic writers. They should be introduced as part of the American experience and not as a different entity.

WB: Which society in the U.S., if there are various societies, do you belong to in your point of view?

RF: I think I belong to the society of my peers.

WB: How would you name them?

RF: I don't know. Maybe intellectuals or pseudointellectuals.

WB: You're phasing out the Cuban aspect totally.

RF: Oh no, no. Cubans are included within that group.

WB: Do you think that not being monolingual is an asset?

RF: Being nonmonolingual? Well, it is and it is not.

WB: Could you explain that?

RF: Well, if you're monolingual, you don't have this constant schizophrenia or debate within you: how to interpret things and in what language to write and what to use. The advantage of being bilingual is that it opens your horizon to so many different types of experiences that otherwise you'll never interpret. I guess it gives you a much more open frame of mind. It doesn't make you more conservative or liberal; it just gives you more experiences.

WB: I always felt that Spanish being the second language in the U.S.—and it is not disappearing; on the contrary, it is augmenting—is an important phenomenon, and people who are both Spanish- and English-speaking could interpret the Latin American and the Caribbean experience to the Anglo population. In other words, they are an element that could be extremely useful in mediating between the two worlds, which are very conflicting and different. What do you think?

RF: That is true. But I also see that the U.S. has become more Latin with all these people—there is a Latinization of the United States. So I think, as times goes on, the United States will become, more than the rest of the Americas, more heterogeneous.

WB: Do you see the "English only" laws as a reaction against Cubans in the U.S.?

RF: I saw that as a reaction against Cubans making it too fast. That was the only way to slap them back. One thing is to welcome a few refugees; another is when the refugees take over. One says, "Hey, how can we get back at these people?"

WB: Where are your national loyalties? That is a very complex thing, I know.

RF: Well, I think the Spanish serves better to define, say, my *país*. My *país* is the United States. My *patria* is Cuba. You make the difference in Spanish. In English you can't because they're both the same, and it's not the same as homeland. Of course, I haven't been to my *patria* in many years, and whenever I go back I may decide that it's the other way around.

WB: Did you ever go back?

RF: No, I haven't been back. I think I don't want to go back.

WB: That's depressing, but it is interesting.

RF: Right. But I have so many different fantasies. I'm bothered that they might be destroyed. I mean, I probably think my grandfather's house was a castle, and I go there and it's just a house, you know. I tried to go last year with this friend of mine. We were doing an article for an outdoor magazine. I asked for a visa, and I never heard from them because, you know, we have to go there with a Cuban passport. Before it was the Czechoslovakian embassy that issued it; now it's the Swiss embassy, but it's only valid for Cuba.

WB: Now culturally, where would you situate yourself? And where emotionally?

RF: I have mixed emotions. About everything. Sometimes I feel part of this and sometimes I feel, shit, I'm no part of this.

WB: What language do you speak at home?

RF: Spanish, sometimes English.

WB: But more Spanish than English with your family?

RF: Oh yes, more Spanish because we want the girls to learn Spanish. That's an effort we make. It takes a lot of energy. Sometimes they just answer you back in English, and you have to hammer in the Spanish.

WB: What is the natural language you converse in with your wife?

RF: Spanish, unless we are talking about technical things we learned in school. Then we switch to English.

WB: Do you feel a special allegiance to Third World issues or Caribbean issues? Or a special sensitivity to what is happening in that part of the world?

RF: I keep up usually with what is happening in Cuba, of course, because I listen to the Cuban radio in Tallahassee, and I keep up with what is happening in Puerto Rico and in the Dominican Republic and with what people are thinking there. I am more interested in what happens in Cuba and Puerto Rico than what is happening in Minnesota.

WB: I can see that. As you know, 1992 is a commemorative date. What do you feel about these five hundred years? What kind of celebration would you endorse?

RF: Oh yes, I'll endorse it—maybe a party or a celebration.

WB: Well, what do you think about Columbus and the *conquista*?

RF: Columbus was trying to make it. And the way he tried to make it was to find a new route to the Indies and get some glory. He wanted to become some sort of hidalgo.

WB: Yes, he wanted to become rich. You have written and published both in Spanish and in English. How do you see the situation of getting published in Spanish in the U.S.? What kind of market is there? What kind of publishing service? What are the problems and the potential?

RF: The problem is that it is a limited market. It could have potential, but a lot of the people that come are rural people, and they don't have a good command of Spanish anyway. The Cuban refugees of '59 and the sixties were for the most part educated, and there was a flourishing literature. It is the anti-Castro and nostalgic literature which filled many libraries in Miami.

WB: Could you mention a few of the publishing houses that publish in Spanish?

RF: In Miami it is Universal. That's the one that publishes. And there was a Betania, which also was in Spain, and there were small presses.

WB: Is Linden Lane still alive?

RF: Yes, Linden Lane publishes out of Princeton, not the university but the town. But those came later on. Right before or after the Mariel boat lift, which brought another type of writer.

WB: Could you mention some names?

RF: I think at the time probably there were Reinaldo Arenas and Jesús Barquet. Then there was Roberto Valero out of Washington, and then you have Herberto Padilla. But those were essentially Cuban writers writing in the United States, so they don't like to hear that. I mean they could have been in Zimbabwe or in Paris and still be essentially Cuban writers.

WB: There's also, of course, a Bilingual Press in Tempe, Arizona.

RF: But before, those presses were shy with Cubans. Chicanos considered us right-wing and extremely conservative.

WB: Since when did Cuban writers get published by Bilingual Press and Arte Público in Houston?

RF: I think it started in the early eighties.

WB: So the Cuban publishing circle was a rather closed one.

RF: Right. It existed only in Miami per se and somewhat in New Jersey. But mostly in Miami.

WB: Why do you think this opened up in the early eighties?

RF: I think it opened up because some of these presses had government grants, and to look good they needed to expand their category of writers.

WB: How do you see your function as a writer in an American and Cuban-American society?

RF: I think my first concern is my craft, and then it is what I write about, which is Cuban-American, because that is what I know.

WB: For whom do you write?

RF: I write mostly for people of my generation. They are between two worlds, and if the rest of the other people read it, that's a plus.

WB: Would you also say what many writers have said and are saying: "I write for myself first"?

RF: Well, I have fun writing for myself. Then one always says: "I'm surprised that people read it." [*Laughter.*] Because when I wrote *Raining Backwards,* I had a very agreeable time. I laughed and I was having a good time with it. It's a tragicomedy, so it has some sad parts to it also.

WB: Let's get back to the politics of American publishing. How difficult is it to enter into what I call the mythical mainstream?

RF: It is very difficult, even for people who are not of ethnic background, because that's mostly controlled by the Northeast. And maybe a little bit in California. It's difficult, so if you have an ethnic component—if you say Fernández or whatever—they already have a prejudice about it. It's not easy. Now, there have been some Cuban-Americans, you know; after Oscar Hijuelos came out with *Mambo Kings,* there was *Dreaming in Cuba* by Christina Garcia, and there's Virgil Suarez. But they are mostly about families and the American Dream. It could be Italians or Greeks for that matter.

WB: So is it the classical immigrant story that big publishers want?

RF: And if you throw in any other curve there, you're out.

WB: Well, that's publishing politics. Would you say that there is a clear generational shift within Cuban-American writing between your generation and the older writers?

RF: Yes. A break with them was using English. That was a major break. The younger Cuban writer has a little bit of nostalgia about a place he has never seen or hardly remembers. Then with the younger generations coming up, I am sure there will be an echo of Cuba there, but it will probably get dimmer and dimmer as time passes. They might use it to add some sort of spice, like some writers use cute little French words.

WB: Let us get back to Miami, which is a kind of city-state and home territory for you. What are the values or the emotions of Cuban life that to you are so appealing? And Cubans are, of course, not the only group that lives there. We'll get to that in a second step.

RF: You know, you feel that there is life there. People are lively, and they sit in the streets; they yell and they scream and they fight. In other Anglo cities it's pretty much like at five o'clock you're dead, you know. And in Miami there are people loving and hating and everything else. It's a very bubbly type of place. You feel that there is something going on there. Good or bad, but it's going on. And that's what I like about it. And then what I told you before—that people have shared the same experiences. I talk to them and I don't have to explain things. They know what I'm talking about. It's very important. And the joking. You can joke without explaining things.

WB: Now, Miami is also known for great racial tensions. Why, according to you, do these tensions exist? They are mainly between Cubans and blacks, Cubans and Jews, Cubans and Puerto Ricans—or how do you see the constellation?

RF: With the blacks there is tension because they resent the Cuban community. The government helped the Cubans because we fled a Communist nation. There is also tension between the Cubans and the blacks because the United States teaches the immigrants who come in to be racist.

WB: How do they do that?

RF: Well, because you do not want to be associated with the people at the bottom, because you are trying to go up, so you shun any group that you perceive as second-rate. It's going to be a drawback to you. And I think many people do it. In New York the conflict is with the blacks and the Italians and the Irish. So I think the Cubans are no different. And especially since most of the Cubans who left Cuba were white Cubans.

WB: Well, the Marielitos had quite a few blacks.

RF: Right.

WB: And criminals also.

RF: And criminals also. Right. So they were appalled, you know.

WB: That was the other Cuba.

RF: Right. And they would say, "Well, these people don't look like Cubans. They don't look like us! Something went wrong in Cuba! What happened there?"

WB: But they must have known that. You know that this existed.

RF: Yes, but I guess they forgot. [*Laughs.*]

WB: How would you judge the *convivencia* between Cubans and blacks in Miami?

RF: Oh, there is no *convivencia*. They tell you something like "Be careful when you drive that way because that becomes black after such and such a street" and things like that. The government tries to say we are going to have these cultural meetings, to alleviate tensions, but I don't see that resolved anytime soon.

WB: So, actually, when we talk about multiculturalism and apply it to Miami, which you know best, it's actually a sham, if that infers harmony.

RF: You have multiculturalism because we get a lot of Central Americans.

WB: That's basically within one cultural root.

RF: And as long as the Cubans are managing the show, they have no problem. The Cubans are very prejudiced.

WB: So what we actually have is a juxtaposition of cultures that are considered unequal.

RF: Unequal, right.

WB: So it's not multiharmonious. Is this mythical?

RF: There is no harmony right now. Maybe in a hundred years from now.

WB: How do you situate yourself in the Cuban-American writing tradition after '59?

RF: I think I follow, more or less, the tradition of Cabrera Infante. There is not that much of the Menippean type of tradition in Latin American literature. But I am also influenced by North American writers. I also think of Vonnegut. I've read all of his stuff. I like him.

WB: I can see that. When you started out writing, in which language did you write?

RF: In Spanish.

WB: What was your first publication, not book publication but short publication? Do you remember?

RF: That was 1974.

WB: What was it?

RF: I think it was "La Llamada," which appeared in a journal, in one of those little Cuban journals that had to do with municipalities of Cuba and exile and things like that. And then I came to *Cuentos sin rumbos*.

WB: Were you from the start critical or at least humorous, if not satirical, of Cubans in the U.S.?

RF: Yes, I was. I thought they were taking themselves too seriously, you know. People should learn to laugh about themselves. And I thought it was time to get a little humor and a little satire here and there and let these people relax from this euphoria—the anti-Communism, the anti-this and the anti-that, Castro and all the campaigns.

WB: I find this is one of the main thrusts of your writing—critique, contentiousness, and well, conspiracy mentalities. The other one is a criticism of American consumerism, which is pushed very hard on any immigrant to begin with but which the middle- and upper-class Cubans took up beautifully. In fact, they exaggerated it even. Would you agree to that?

RF: Yes, I agree to that because they already knew all these things from Cuba, because we were so close to the United States. So they didn't have to push them too hard. They were already a converted crowd.

WB: And they knew the products!

RF: Yes, they knew everything. Now there's a television show in Miami called *Sábado Gigante* that is, I think, very sad. I don't like it because of what they do to the audience there. Here comes this nice beautiful woman, coming with whatever product, and the audience sings this jingle: "Let's buy; *compremos* Charmin." [*Sings tune.*] So they are indoctrinating the people to buy all these products. It could be oil; it could be whatever.

WB: What is part of the more formal Cuban culture in Miami? Are there theaters?

RF: Yes, there are a lot of theaters. Well, the theaters still cater to the anti-Communist thing or an obsession with homosexuality. And there is another group that does a serious type of stuff, but that is within the universities.

WB: You had from the start in your writing relatively short entities, which went also into *Raining Backwards*. Why those short entities?

RF: Well, in *Raining Backwards* I wanted to portray some type of chaos, and that was the best way to do it. And also maybe because I don't think linearly, maybe that has something to do with it. I don't like to write linear stuff. I would rather go into the next unit and develop that one later on and keep going and going.

WB: Which is also a postmodern type of writing. In *La vida es un special* you satirize a lot—consumerism, that's the most evident element of satire probably. Also pretentiousness about not having the right servants.

RF: Yes, because they are telling you all that. The people who were middle class in Cuba keep inflating themselves. Some of these people themselves were servants, but now they can rewrite their history because they are in a new place.

WB: You could even say that this is the American story. You leave the old country and you can reshape yourself, reinvent yourself. It is a lie, if you insist on the factual, but it is also a great opportunity. Wouldn't you say that in a close-knit society like the Cuban one everybody knew that this was a little tenant family and not a family of landowners?

RF: Right. Well, the other people just talk about it, but these people don't have the economic power nor the means to fight it, so they just say, "I am in the group." But then the other ones just keep shining I guess. I was in a funeral once, and this woman said to another woman: "Oh, where are you from in Cuba?" She said, "I am from Havana." And the other woman added, "From where?" and she said, "From Miramar," and then the other woman answered, "So am I, from Eighty-third." And then this other woman said, "I'm from Miramar too, and there was no Eighty-third Street, it ended in Eighty-second."

WB: There we go.

RF: I love to go to the Quince Años. The parameters for the Quince Años that were set by the Cuban high bourgeoisie were broken, so there were no more people for that. The Quince was just a coming-out party. Now the U.S. gives them a chance. I mean, if you were a carpenter or something, all you need is to be rich or efficient.

WB: Reading your first two books I had the impression that you were recording a culture with some affection, and nostalgia as well, but that's rather traditional I'd say.

RF: Right. They were not threatening.

WB: Now, the second one, *La vida es un special,* was already much more critical.

RF: The reception was rather negative. The criticism was that I was pink, people would write. I have a couple of nasty letters there; I kept a few. They would say, "Why do you criticize us so much" or "Why do you do this? Are you trying to portray the wrong image of us?" That's what a woman told me once.

WB: For me, that is one of the difficult points of ethnic writing—that there is a group pressure that the Anglo writer does not have because the ethnic in-group has expectations that you are supposed to meet.

RF: Right.

WB: And you are crucified if you don't. It happened to Baldwin; it happened to virtually everyone. On the other hand, it is great stuff for satire. Now, what are some of the procedures, the literary techniques of satire as you see them and use them?

RF: I use hyperbole. That's probably my main technique. I see

La montaña ruse to a certain extent as a special study for *Raining Backwards*. You know, like a painter has different studies. That's the way I see it.

WB: *Raining Backwards,* I think, had a great impact and was a breakthrough for you, wouldn't you say?

RF: Yes, it was.

WB: Could you comment on the reinventing of a world in *Raining Backwards*?

RF: Well, everybody there is trying to remember, but as time passes, remembrances become fantasies; and the more they try to remember, the further away they get from the reality of what it was like. So at the end what you have is a complete mythical ending with the reinvention of their past.

WB: At the same time, because you don't want to write a traditional naturalistic or realistic novel, you don't furnish the facts and the background; you leave that out. So what we get is actually the fictionalizing, the mythifying of Mirta's figures in Miami and Cuba.

RF: Yes, that's what I had in mind.

WB: And you mix discourses like letters, monologues . . . This mythifying is also very much an immigrant's attitude.

RF: Well, you don't understand how this society works, so in order to find some sort of place you have to create all this mythology. Myths were created to explain what you don't understand.

WB: You know I laughed a lot reading the novel, but it is also a very sad story.

RF: Yes, it is a tragicomedy.

WB: Yes, because you see people on the verge of going to pieces.

RF: Right. I always see it as a New Orleans carnival or as a sort of happy funeral, but it is still a funeral. There is a lot of pageantry, but you are getting ready to bury someone. Some people don't see that. Some people just see the comic aspects of it.

WB: Would you say that Cuban culture, island culture, is not only transforming itself on the mainland but is vanishing?

RF: Yes, I do. Sometimes I write a dedication for someone, and it says, "Welcome to the world of Mirta—a vanishing nebula." Many of the kids prefer to use English, which is a clash with my generation or the older generations, who primarily communicate in Spanish.

WB: But Cubans have the reputation of being almost arrogant and very sure of themselves. Do they see the Anglo world as superior even to themselves? I don't have that impression.

RF: No, they don't, but it's sort of trendy. That's the way they see it.

WB: I was mentioning the term *Hispanic,* which is, along with *multiculturalism,* something that pops up in that context. What are your feelings about this term, which I assume was used for university purposes, for—

RF: . . . government purposes. I mean I have to use the term because I have no other word, and the government has the word, and you have to fill it in. *Hispanic* may be—eighty or a hundred years from now—a valid term, when there is some sort of group consciousness about being Hispanic. But right now I don't like to use it because it denies what I am. You know, I'm a Cuban or a Cuban-American; and if you say I'm Hispanic, it denies me my whole Cuban culture. Everything that I was taught to retain by my parents this new term takes away from me—my literature, the history that I learned as a child when I went to school in Cuba. And then they harp always on the race. The black, white, and Hispanic races. Hispanic is not a race. It's a cultural group or a make-believe entity.

WB: What is the influence of Cuban music in your work?

RF: There is a lot of influence of pop culture, of Cuban music like salsa and Latin American music, in the work. I use it in *Raining Backwards* for, you know, Dr. King's letter writings. Her advice is usually coming from Cuban or American songs or songs from Julio Iglesias—syrupy types of things. That is the type of advice that she gives, so I like to use it that way. I like to use intertextuality a lot. Like, Conny's suicidal notice comes from Sor Juana Inés de la Cruz, but it is in English and in the voice of a cheerleader.

WB: It is lost on those readers who don't have the cultural background.

RF: The discourse for the monolingual who reads this book is limited. If a bilingual reads it, he can enjoy it on a different level. The other one might find it exotic or whatever and doesn't understand it. Maybe the Anglo world imposes the language. What we do with the language is play with it, and so we give him the things in English he can't understand. It is like somebody said, encoding and decoding the message.

WB: When you think back on those three days here in Erlangen with writers from other cultural backgrounds and their attitudes toward America and American society, toward American cultures, can you draw any conclusions from your experience?

RF: I think everybody was trying to write about their own territory and personal niche within the culture, but within American culture, and we're a part of it the way I see it. I mean I could relate a lot to Grace [Paley]. Some other people I could not. I could relate to Luci [Tapahonso] and the longing and certain things which she is trying to retrieve but less to Ed [Vega], in the sense that he's much more militant; and for me that's sort of a foreign concept because in Miami I never grew up with it.

WB: Your family was not militant in a political way?

RF: No.

WB: No? They just withdrew from that?

RF: Completely. Some of my uncles are political, but my father and my mother, no, they withdrew into the hinterlands or whatever [*laughs*], which was good because then I could see Miami like a circus, observe it from many angles. Had I lived there, I would have been swallowed by the whole vortex because it can really swallow you like the sea.

WB: Joan Didion wrote a book about Miami called *Miami*. It is an interesting book in that it reeks of conspiracies and groups of Cubans conspiring against each other, against the government, the government against certain groups, and so on.

RF: Everybody wants to be first in the pecking order there.

WB: Yes, and they always suspect that somebody is a spy. It creates difficult human relations. [*Both laugh.*]

TWO

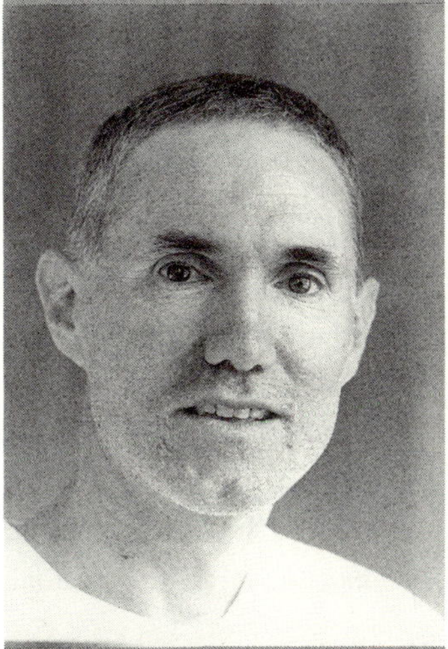

ANDREW HOLLERAN

interviewed by Christina Strobel

The Anglo-American Andrew Holleran, born in 1944, is a novelist and an essayist; he is one of the first prominent American authors to address male homosexuality in literature. He received much critical praise for his novels Dancer from the Dance *(1978), which has already become a classic, and* Nights in Aruba *(1983), both of which have been translated into German. His perceptive essays on AIDS and other contemporary issues have been collected in* Ground Zero *(1989). Holleran studied at Harvard University; today he lives in Florida. The New York City milieu provides the essential setting for both of his novels. His fiction portrays gay life often from a tragic angle, but there is also much humor and sympathy for his characters.*

CS: I noticed that in both of your novels, *Dancer from the Dance* and *Nights in Aruba,* the protagonists have very similar memories of their childhood. In both cases the father is of German descent and rather . . . distant . . .

AH: Cold.

CS: Cold and distant. And the mother is just the opposite.

AH: Right.

CS: And she comes from Chicago in both books. She's of a Catholic-Irish family. The boy spends some time in Chicago, then grows up in the tropics, where the father goes for an engineering job. In both novels the mother has more drinks than the boy, who is in both novels called a puritan, likes her to have. She reads murder mysteries, and in both books mother and son go to mass on Sundays, the mother wearing gloves. [*Laughs.*] Even the memories coincided in some close details, as in their relationship to the father. The father comes home from the office in his white shirt that "bears the odor of air conditioning." The boy guards his sleep after lunch . . .

AH: *Stop!*

CS: I'm not finished.

AH: *Stop!*

CS: Wait! And another thing that was really interesting too. The father says of a painting in the dining room, and I quote . . .

AH: Is that in both books?

CS: Wait.

AH: That's how I want my family to be?

CS: A painting "of a woman knitting in an apple orchard outside a whitewashed hut while her children played at her feet" [*Nights in Aruba*: 26] or "of a woman knitting in a grove of fruit trees while her children played about her skirts" [*Dancer from the Dance*: 60]. And this is how he wants his family, right?

AH: I'm not doing this interview.

CS: No? [*Laughs.*]

AH: Take me back. [*Both laugh.*] I had no idea there were that many correspondences. I was surprised by what you're saying. I didn't even know it was that close, but you're absolutely right. And I have no defense for that fact except that you write out of your own life. Obviously, it's autobiographical.

CS: Well, I wouldn't have known.

AH: Right. What were you going to ask me about it? Why the similarities?

CS: Yes. Why? I was getting confused, and I thought, well, maybe these are the same people after all. But it can't be. One is Malone, the other's Paul, and they're not that similar. But their childhood is . . .

AH: I have no defense for that except that obviously you keep writing about the things that matter to you over and over again. The thing about my second book that bothered me in a way was that it was a mixture of autobiography and imagination, which I don't think I quite decided on; whereas *Dancer,* for some reason from its structure, was always a work that I thought of as a story I was making up of characters I was making up. The second book I began to start writing much more autobiographically. So, obviously, I just used that childhood material again because it mattered to me, and I did it in the I-narrator rather than ascribing it to a third-person character.

CS: Well, the obvious question . . .

AH: But, you know, the horrible thing about it is I was thinking about the next book I'm trying to write. And I was thinking I still haven't got this right. I still haven't got this right. And I thought, I'm going to do this one more time and get this right. But that's crazy. There's a writer in America called Louis Auchincloss who wrote an essay called "A Writer's Capital." And he says that all writers have certain memories, a certain life experience that is their capital, and that they use this as they write over their life. And I think that in a sense it's absolutely true, and the real danger of writing is to use your capital because you can only spend it once, in a way, after people ask you questions like these especially. There's a book by J. R. Ackerley, a British writer, called *My Father and Myself,* which is his autobiographical book. And it's just a masterpiece I think. It's brilliantly done. But he kept that book—he worked on that book for twenty to thirty years, and it wasn't even published until after he died because he kept getting it right, and in a sense, that's correct. You really only have one chance to tell that story that everybody has in them, and you should do it in a way that is good. It's a riot.

CS: It did make me wonder about your childhood.

AH: All of it is right there. Yes. That's where the title of *Nights in Aruba* comes from. I actually grew up in Aruba, and the day I found out that was going to be the title I put it on the manuscript and sent it to my editor because they wanted a book from me—a second book. It was very hard for me to write a second book. You never know why your first book was liked. You don't know whether you're supposed to do the same thing again, if you can do something radically different, if you will disappoint your readers, if they understood the first book and you should make it more clear what your feelings are about things in another way. So I was very hesitant about sending this book in. I sent it in, and that was a working title. They accepted it. They put it into the process of being published and told me one day that that was the title. And I nearly dropped the telephone because I didn't want it to be so nakedly autobiographical, but that *is* exactly where I grew up. Those were the circumstances. Chicago, Ohio, from my parents' background. Watching the telephone when my father took a nap. The drinking, the listening to the mother talk in the evenings, the mass. All of that. Those were all literal . . .

CS: *And* the painting?

AH: And the painting, which is now in the house in Florida. That painting is still there. But that's a very important painting, really, because in a sense a lot of the criticism I have of gay life or the longing in a lot of my work is for this domestic peace with this kind of ideal domestic life, which, I think, is very hard for a lot of gay men to attain, and it interests me as to why that is. And then you have to ask yourself whether it's a romantic picture or whether it's something that's really attainable in life at all.

CS: Why is the father not in that picture?

AH: Good question.

CS: This is his ideal family, and he's not in there?

AH: My father has subsequently died since the second book, and the strongest thing in the book I'm working on now is about his death, and I'm thinking to myself, this is the subject that I should keep going with. So it will deal with the father. Somebody said the book about your father is the book that everybody has to write. But in real life my father was a kind of distant, mysterious—not unfriendly but not demonstrative—person, so what I know about my father is probably much less than what I know about my mother. But again I'm faced with the same problem of whether to do it as fiction or as fact.

CS: Well, *Nights in Aruba* is a mixture of both?

AH: Exactly. But I think that's unsatisfactory. I think you should either do one or the other and not—no, I don't know; I can't decide. I think it's an issue. It's a difficult issue. I was saying to Grace Paley that since writing the essays I've developed this comfortable I-narrator, this person who is speaking in the essays, and it's so easy to write. This voice. I feel so comfortable with it now that when it came time to start a novel, and I started writing in the I-narrator again, I had to say to myself, well, who is *this* I-narrator? Grace said to me, "Oh, you have to make up an I-narrator who is completely different, someone you may hate or something," which is what they always told us in writing school, but I've never, never liked that technique.

CS: Why do the narrators in your novels either not have a name or get named very late? The narrator in *Dancer from the Dance* says at the beginning that he did not change any names, that there were no innocents to protect, but he never gives his own—or I missed it.

AH: No, no. You're absolutely right.

CS: The narratee, the person the story is told to, the narratee in this novel signs the last of the framing letters with "Paul." That really struck me. Is that some kind of conclusion? Is he coming to terms with himself? And what about the other Paul, in *Nights in Aruba,* who gets named—of all people and of course—by his mother. For him that means that she conceives of him as a separate person, and he doesn't seem pleased. He's still traveling on the passport they shared since when he was a kid. He gets named by his mother, and it's an act he . . .

AH: Resists.

CS: Yes, he resists.

AH: I didn't notice that. My reason for that is, I think, that for some instinctual reason I like the narrator to remain a ghost—not a character, just an observer. I don't even want to create a narrator at all. There's a book by Turgenev called *A Sportsman's Sketches* in which he travels around the Russian countryside hunting. He sees peasants and he tells their stories—that's kind of my idea. The narrator is not important. He's just a storyteller, and so I say to myself, why do you need a narrator at all? And I don't know why because I like the first person. It's more immediate. And I do want the author's voice, but I don't want the narrator to be a separate character. I want him to remain unnamed. I can't explain. There's a wonderful moment in Proust when Proust draws attention to the narrator and says, "If you think this is really me . . ."—kind of saying it doesn't matter.

CS: Did your parents know about your life in New York?

AH: No. Part of the good thing about my family was that they allowed freedom. Everyone was able to pursue his own course, and they did *not* ask questions. I liked that in a way, but the negative side of that was, it was part of this . . . distance. It was the good side of something that was also in a way bad. But I don't criticize anybody for this. Anyway, so did they know about my life in New York? I will never know if they knew the specifics of it. I've discussed this with my sister, and we've asked each other whether we think my father knew about my gay life, and neither one of us can be sure. It was never explicitly discussed. I think I baffled him. I think he did not know if I was happy or not because I had not done the usual things to achieve happiness. I had not gotten married. I had not gotten the kind of job he'd had, so I think he was baffled. But I also think he assumed that I was doing what I wanted, and he wasn't going to interfere.

I went to law school and dropped out—and it was so funny the night I phoned my parents and told them I was leaving law school because I wanted to write instead, and they said, "All right, now, we just want you to be happy." I hung up the phone, and I thought "What!? Is that all? They really don't care? They just want me to be happy?" I had been doing so many things—consciously or subconsciously as we all do, with what our parents would think of what we were doing. So I was really amazed. But I do in the end think that that's probably all parents want for their children, that they be happy in whatever way they want to be.

CS: What do you think of outing?

AH: I had to write an article on outing for a magazine that folded, and it was not printed. I interviewed Michelangelo Signorile, who was the guy who did it at *Outweek Magazine*. He had a column, and every week he would try to out somebody. He was the one that all the television talk shows interviewed when it became an issue in the press. I did a little research. I wrote the article, and then I ended it with a funeral I went to, of my best friend in New York. And we were sitting at the memorial service in this auditorium at a university in New York. He was a college professor, a wonderful teacher, and his mother and his sister were in the front row, and everyone got up and spoke about him—what a wonderful teacher he was. The students got up. Colleagues got up and everything, and not a word was said about his gayness or his gay friends. And I went home afterward, and I thought to myself it was good that nobody got up and said anything like that because it might have offended the mother and the sister. But why would it have been offensive or inconsiderate to say that if there's nothing wrong with it? And so I ended the essay with that scene, and when my editor called back he said, "You know, you're in favor of outing." I said, "No, no, I'm not. I think it's awful. I don't think anybody can do that to anybody else." He said,

"No, you're in favor of it." So obviously I have mixed feelings about it.

The illogic of it is, if there's nothing wrong with being homosexual, there is nothing wrong with saying someone is homosexual. Obviously, there is something wrong with saying someone is homosexual. It can cost them their job. It can expose them to violence. It can endanger their relations with their family, with their friends, with their school. So the facts of life are that it potentially is a very damaging piece of information. The argument of the outers is to say the reason it is damaging is because everyone is not out; and if everyone was out, the society would see the scope of homosexuality and there would be nothing wrong with being gay. It's the chicken or the egg argument. Which do you do first?

I think in the end you come down to the human value, which is, I can't do it in my gut. The best argument against it is that it's a person's privilege to divulge information about himself when he wants and where he wants and to whom he wants. You can argue up and down for days, but I would say the whole issue has subsided. I found in my research that even when Michelangelo would try to out people, the press, the mainstream press in the United States, would not do it because they consider it a code of ethics not to out somebody. There were in fact only two people, organizations, that were outing people at the time this started. One was *Outweek,* and the other was a tabloid newspaper called *The National Enquirer.* Do you have an opinion on outing?

CS: I think it's every person's business to give this information or keep it. And it's too dangerous really. How can someone dare take the risk of hurting someone or their family—I mean, you can't calculate the risk you are taking; you don't know what the actual consequences might be. It may be good for the cause—and I even doubt that—but what's first? I think a person has to decide for himself or herself when she's ready to do that, to say that, to live that.

AH: I do too. I do too. The irony of AIDS is that AIDS has been an enormous example of outing. AIDS has brought gay life into the mainstream in a way that nothing else did.

CS: You said AIDS and homosexuality are being equated very much in the States?

AH: They are, yes.

CS: It's not really a homosexual disease only, though. There are hemophiliacs. There are heterosexuals and children. There are people who had blood transfusions after an operation and . . .

AH: And in Africa it's by far a heterosexual disease, and it amazes me that there is so little coverage of that fact. It's as if nobody cares about that and AIDS. Yes, you're absolutely right, and in New York the percentage now has shifted too, I think; it's less gay than drug addicts and other categories. But let's face it, it began in the gay population, and it has wreaked an enormous amount of damage there. And it has changed gay life and affected gay people, gay men again, more directly and more at the root of what they are than anything else, than any other group. Oh, that's not fair. Think of this thing going on in France now. It's incredible.

CS: In your essays you call AIDS the plague. What else? The bomb. IT. Capital *I, T.* Why isn't there more resistance to this equation of homosexuality with disease? Or more generally, how is AIDS treated in gay writing? Is death/the fatal disease seen as a consequence of forbidden love or as blind fate? And is writing about it possible? Except in what you call a new genre, the obituaries.

AH: AIDS is being treated in gay writing now, but in some way I still think it is impossible. Officially, rationally, one is supposed to say AIDS is blind fate, a microbiological accident, but I think in reality there is a large residue of guilt and shame (over promiscuity and being gay) that AIDS plays into. No one has dealt with that yet. Rationally, it is an accident, but emotionally it is still a terrible consequence of being gay, I suspect, for many people.

CS: In your essays you say that AIDS really changed people, not just sex. You said that one of the major changes was that gay people, gay men, were learning to help each other. "We are discovering the strength and goodness of people we knew only in discotheques or as faces on Fire Island" [*Ground Zero*: 42].

AH: I did say that. I did say that.

CS: Clam in *Nights in Aruba* says, "Out of this dreadful disease, perhaps something good will come. We are treating each other like human beings again. Not like hamburger" [233].

AH: I think the response that gay men brought to AIDS, and things like the Gay Men's Health Crisis, and all the amazing work that was done also benefited nongay people with AIDS. All the structures and the pressure, the political pressure that these groups initiated in the beginning of the plague are still in place, and they're now helping women and Hispanics and drug addicts. Those structures are permanent, and they're now helping other groups, but the gay men who started them deserve credit for what they did. And it gained them respect in the population at large, and it certainly gave them self-respect too. So, yes, it did change people. On the other hand I am absolutely amazed at the fact that I don't think AIDS has changed the psychology of homosexuality or American homosexual life at all. I was talking to someone here this afternoon who said it's caused more monogamy and more couples among gay men in Erlangen and Nürnberg; and theoretically that's what was supposed to have happened in America too, but I don't think it has to the degree that they expected. I think that there are just things that do not change at all. People cruise, and the way they trick and the way they form or don't form relationships—that's fascinating to me because if AIDS couldn't change that I can't imagine what will. So there must be something very structural about it all that is just resistant to any kind of idealism or any kind of cultural condition.

CS: Maybe this *is* the cultural condition? For a certain group among the gay men?

AH: Right, right. But then it should be addressed and recognized as such, and people should ask why—which they don't very often.

CS: Well, I think we're getting to where I had lots of problems with your books.

AH: Okay.

CS: Right. I don't know how I can even talk about this, but it seems to me—and I may have misunderstood this totally . . .

AH: Here comes a *tough one*!

CS: [*Laughs.*]

AH: Good.

CS: Now, male homosexuality, at least as it is described for a certain group in *Dancer,* seems to operate along a certain set of rules. And the rules are, at least in this book . . .

AH: Go ahead.

CS: . . . for this group . . . Okay, there's an ideal of masculinity, and it's measured by the size of the penis . . .

AH: Right.

CS: . . . by standards of physical beauty . . .

AH: Right.

CS: . . . by a compulsion to have as much sex as possible with absolutely no obligations . . .

AH: Right.

CS: . . . or attachment, and that is then seen as sexual liberation, right?

AH: [*Laughs.*]

CS: Well, it *could* be called sexual liberation. It *is* in a way. But what is beyond me is how any behavior that is finally based on oppressive standards can lead to liberation. It seems that these standards of masculinity have been swallowed whole by this group, and in their indigestion they've raised them to a higher power, and now they use them as their own. I don't think this can do anyone good. It's the same with sex. Sex is what was used to marginalize these people, right? And so this is what they place at the very center of their lives. In a way it's a reaction that makes sense, and also, sex may have anarchist tendencies. It's a reaction to what excludes you, and it could be subversive. So it makes sense in a way, but then, if you just accept what the oppressive rules are and claim them as your own, I don't think it will change your life very much.

AH: Why . . . what do you mean when you say that it was used to marginalize people?

CS: Because it was the "wrong" kind of sexuality. There are only certain kinds of sexuality that are acceptable in society. Right? You've got to be in a heterosexual marriage and have 2.3 kids.

AH: I was thinking to myself, even on the panel, what did I as a gay man have in common with a Native American, a black man, et cetera, et cetera. I thought to myself, in a sense we're all outside the reproductive arena of the main group. Our sense is not to reproduce ourselves as a . . .

CS: That's too easy.

AH: Okay. Go ahead. Fine.

CS: No, really. There are lots of heterosexuals who don't want to reproduce. One. There are homosexuals who live with . . .

AH: But don't you think . . . wait! Stop! Stop! Stop! Let me finish. Don't you think they are looked at askance? That they are less respected than a heterosexual couple that does have a family?

CS: That's true, generally.

AH: I think it is all based on that one model, and that is something which is very primal, which is simply continuing the race, continuing the genes, providing for the next generation.

CS: Right. Well, maybe.

AH: And I think if you can examine adultery from that viewpoint, you can examine all reprimands and all disapprobation from that central point. The problem is . . .

CS: The institution of heterosexuality plus reproduction.

AH: Yes.

CS: Yes, but you don't have to accept that. I smiled when I read about all this in one of your essays.

AH: But I don't think people are as free as you think. I do not think anyone is really free. I don't think anyone escapes the programming at some level. A few people may but not many. And I think one of the issues that you're getting at—as to why gay men take the masculine ideal and seem to oppress each other with it—is the fact that they're not free of it either. Go ahead. What were you going to say?

CS: Well, I don't believe in total freedom, but I think there's lots of room for resistance.

AH: Not except in the heterosexual ideal. Yes, and that's what's going on now I think.

CS: So should I read . . .

AH: That's what Quayle is arguing about in the United States, and Bush in an interview in the *New York Times* saying that he does think the basic unit has to be a man and a woman and that the children deserve parents of both sexes. That is still a very widely held view. And they are entitled to hold that view. The point is, if you do not practice that system, can you free yourself of the ideal yourself? Can you get rid of the internalization of those ideals? Since gay people are not raised to be gay. They're all raised, most of them, in the family, and it's ludicrous to think that they're going to—on becoming gay, on discovering their gayness—not have any effect from those upbringings.

CS: Sure, but lesbians weren't raised to be lesbians and seem to be getting along fine. I wasn't raised to have no kids. So what? But I think resistance is possible.

AH: Yes, I agree with you. And I agree with you also to the extent that therefore gay men should look at their lives and say, in what ways are we not free of this stuff? There's one theory that all gay life is nothing more than a working out of shame, and sometimes you can look at why gay men do not attach obligations or anything more permanent to a sexual encounter, for example. Why are gay men involved in this thing of tricking? One argument is that they're male and that biologically males are this way. It is the female that wants to cohabit or to attach herself—[*CS protests*] okay, I'll just throw all this out. [*Laughs.*]

Another theory is that because nothing comes from the sexual act, no children, there is no reason to stay together. Another idea is that sex is just wonderful, and most people, including heterosexuals, would love to have sex with many more people than they actually do. There's an essay I almost read last night called "Notes on Promiscuity," which goes through all of this.

CS: I really like that one.

AH: I do too. And you can argue it both ways. Who can say what it is? But there is something that is intriguing about the way gay men do behave with one another and why the sex with no strings became such a fundamental characteristic of gay urban life. But also of gay rural life; it's the same in the small towns in Florida where I live. And again, AIDS has not really changed that. And you have to ask yourself why. What was the question originally, though? Oh, you said gay life seems to be deposited on the penis, the muscularity, the masculinity . . .

CS: On the role model that's been given to them by society . . .

AH: The Marlboro Man.

CS: And that's not good for heterosexual or gay men, I feel. That's my problem.

AH: I agree with you completely. I was talking to someone last night who's heterosexual, and he said he'd had identity problems growing up because he was shy and not particularly aggressive, and he had trouble with being male-identified. And I didn't think that if you were straight that that could ever bother you. I always thought that it was being gay that made you depressed about not doing things boys were expected to do. But you're right, it's a problem of masculinity. I just wrote an essay called "Masculinity" in which I tried to address these things, and it was an awful essay. I couldn't get to the bottom of it. It's a very mysterious thing.

CS: It just seems to me that if the role models that are given to us by society don't seem right, if they don't give us room to move, we can construct new ones. We can resist those dominant patterns and institutions. We can try to. I don't think there's total freedom, but there's room we can make for ourselves.

AH: I agree.

CS: So why not find other role models?

AH: I agree. People have done it. That's what the whole gay movement has been, don't you think so? You're saying that there's been partially a step but that they're mirroring too many bad images of what they are supposedly breaking free of.

CS: Well, this model of masculinity, of supermasculinity. That is one I don't understand. So a guy with a short penis can only sit in a corner and be depressed, or what? What about *his* sexual liberation? And then, I also don't understand the other construction that says that a homosexual is really a woman. There's this quote in which homosexuals are compared to women. It says they are "beings whose life consists chiefly of being attractive to others"—that's from *Dancer from the Dance* [248].

AH: Yes.

CS: It seems nothing but a stereotype to me. Feminists have been fighting that for a long time. I don't see it in lesbian relationships; there seems little of the butch and femme role playing nowadays. What is so revolutionary about . . .

AH: I agree with you too, but listen. I think that is still true. I read that coming over on the plane after not having read it a long time. That passage is a little pessimistic perhaps, but I don't think that that is untrue. I was discussing this with a friend this afternoon—the problem of aging as a gay man: when you stop being attractive in a youthful way and you have to realize that you will not be looked at or be able to gain as many partners as you could. And what you use to adjust to that fact with. No one's talking about that except *Death in Venice,* which is extremely pessimistic. But it's part of the fact that with gay men, if homosexuality is essentially about sex and about a sex act that does not lead to anything permanent, then you're constantly having to go out to have this sex again and being attractive is the way you get the sex. Or most people think it is, so you always have to be attractive. And it's kind of hell.

CS: But your definition of being attractive is the problem. It's not that much of a problem for lesbians I think. They don't cling as much to these reductive beauty ideals. Well, at least I like to think so. They're fine. They're old and still love each other.

AH: I agree. And lesbians—we were discussing this too—lesbians are not disqualified because they're older. And I wish more was written about that. Why is that? Why do lesbians have different patterns and values than gay men? You obviously would say it's because men are different from women. What else would you say? It's the old thing about men being attracted by pictures of naked women, but a woman is not necessarily attracted by the pictures of a naked man. She would be attracted by other values about the man. They've done studies like that. I'm not a psychologist, so I shouldn't be talking about this at all, but I do think gay men are trapped unless they have the courage to break out of it. But this friend this afternoon at lunch said that gay American men have much more trouble adjusting to age than Europeans do. He said we're more youth-obsessed and that gay men in America fight it longer because they feel obligated to retain this eternal youth. And I think that's true and that over here it's given in to in a more graceful way. I agree.

CS: Jane Rule in her essays writes about aging. One of her ideas is that women obviously learn different things in life. Women traditionally have had to tend the young, the sick, and the old, so they are more prepared "to extend erotic tenderness against the prevailing horror of aging." So this is maybe one theory.

AH: Yes, yes, I understand. So you're saying the male model is wrong for both straight and gay men. But listen. This is not something that's going to be changed, because if you read Greek literature, the same values were present. And when you read a dialogue of Plato and Socrates, the values were youth, were beauty, or virility. I'm afraid that these things are so encoded that there's no changing in any way. You're speaking in a utopian way.

CS: No.

AH: Well, you tell me what should be attractive in a gay man to other gay men. Tell me. I'll see if I agree with you. Can you answer me?

CS: I don't think so. Plus, I could never say this or that *should* be attractive.

AH: Well, in a less oppressive gay world what would be attractive? It wouldn't be the body?

CS: For women, it's all kinds of things. It's faces, gestures, voices, bodies too, but all kinds of bodies. Physical beauty, yes, but there's a wide range for that. It doesn't need to be the standard that's presented to us by society.

AH: I agree. And one of the things that has happened to me as I've aged that I've liked, one of the things that I think is good about growing older, is that I've absolutely matured in that sense.

I've been able to find beauty in many more kinds of bodies and people than ever before, and I like this very much. And I wish that it was available to people at an earlier age because I don't think it is. When you're young, you're more snobbish, more selective, more hierarchical, you're more localized. But one of the nice things about growing older is that expansion of appreciation of all kinds of people. Absolutely.

CS: And older men can look really . . .

AH: *Absolutely!* As I'm aging and am looking at other men to see how they look, I'm thinking to myself, you know, you *can* look good at that age. Look at this man, et cetera, et cetera.

CS: Well, look at Grace Paley. She'll be turning seventy in December. She looks wonderful.

AH: Right. On the other hand there's a whole time in life, there's a whole segment in society—and it's reflected in advertising and movies and many other things—which says you must look this way, you must be this age, you must have this kind of body. Our talk is useless in a way. Because, as you said, you can't say what one man would find attractive in another man.

CS: Should find attractive.

AH: That's exactly the essence of it. We can talk about what would be better for people psychologically and spiritually and every other way, but we're not going to make a dent I don't think.

CS: Oh, I don't agree.

AH: You think you can make a dent?

CS: If I know what I am doing, if I analyze my behavior patterns and what I see around me, that's the first step to change anything. If you say it won't change, then you say, okay, this is something essentially biologically innate and there's nothing I can do. It's always been like that. I don't think so. That reminds me of something you could explain to me. In your essays you say that a homosexual is a person whose biological identity seems at variance with his sexual one.

AH: Yes.

CS: What does that mean?

AH: I think that if you take the procreation view of sex, that the function of sex is to create offspring, that homosexual sex is . . .

CS: You sound like the pope!

AH: I know. But listen. I think the only way to examine homosexuality is to do devil's advocate and to take the worst, the most extreme antihomosexual position and examine it. I can't stand cheerleading; you know what I mean. You've got to take the worst case against it and then discuss it. So the worst case against homosexuality would be that the function of sex is procreation and that therefore homosexual sex is irrational and can never produce the desired object and that all the chaos and the anarchy and the neurosis in the behavior follows from that simple fact. So it's like a case of bad wiring. It's a machine that just isn't functioning well. And I'm sure, I know, that there are many heterosexuals who view homosexuality in that way—that it's a birth defect, that it's a case of bad wiring. That's what they mean when they say something is unnatural. It's not doing its natural function.

CS: Why take that position? Maybe I misread you, but I thought this is what you really think.

AH: Sometimes I do suspect that. I'm not going to pretend otherwise. Sometimes I do suspect that. Sometimes I find myself going out at night when I'm tired because I *have* to meet someone in a park; and I think to myself, this is just crazy! Why are you doing this? How can you still be doing this? You are never reaching a goal. This is crazy. You must say to yourself either this is thrilling and a pleasure and you like doing this, or you're doing this against your will because you have not completed something, you have not accomplished something, and you are just being tortured by this thing. Who knows? I just don't think you can say for sure either way. You obviously think you can. You would say the pope is wrong. [*CS laughs.*] So what is sex, do you think?

CS: What is sex? Communication.

AH: It's a way of being close to another human being. It's the greatest pleasure. Okay. I agree with that. I agree with that, but I also still want to entertain the other thing too.

CS: I think it's always an act of communication. It may not be good communication, but it always is communication.

AH: I agree. I agree.

CS: And there are different ways of relating to different people. Say I have a brief encounter on the bus, say "Hello." I talk to a lady, or we just smile at each other, and that's it. There are those kinds of pleasant and uncommitted encounters in sex, and there are other kinds. That's all an act of communication. That's my theory.

AH: I agree with you. I would almost say that the chief function of living is the communication. That's the chief pleasure, and that's our nature more than anything else. But if sex is the greatest form of communication, why do gay men not make sex a better form of communication than they do?

CS: I'm not sure if it's the greatest form of communication. It may be in some instances, but sometimes there are other forms that work better.

AH: Okay, it is silly to say one is greater than the other. I agree with you. But let's say it's one of the most intense.

CS: I don't think sex is the most important thing in the world. There are all kinds of different forms of communication that can also be quite intense. It is one of the most. There I agree.

AH: Well, that's another question. There's a phrase in an advertisement in a gay newspaper for a center on Ninth Street in New York that says homosexuality isn't just sex. And it's a discussion group. And every time I see that line, I think to myself, but it is. And in a way you could argue that's all it is, that it isn't integrated with other stuff. So I don't know.

CS: You have that line in your collection of essays, that "it's useless to pretend that sex is *not* at the center of homosexual life" [181]. But you also comment that homosexuality "is more than politics; and more than sex" [180]. What is the "more"? Is homosexuality sex or is it more than sex? You have both lines, don't you? Has your definition of homosexuality changed?

AH: That's my problem. I can never decide on things. It's always . . .

CS: I think that means being close to the truth. Most things are contradictory, and you just have to live with paradoxes. I think the more contradiction you have in your life, the more things you're probably doing right.

AH: Do you think so?

CS: Yes. I think society is spoonfeeding us so much, role models and all kinds of weird ideas. So we have to live with those in our minds and bodies, and we often have to bear the contradiction between what we are actually doing and what we think is right, or should be right. So you're bound to have these contradictions all the time. We had better learn to live with them. Or what about enjoying them? They point to options—no?

AH: Well, I'm thinking, though, it's even worse in the sense that every thesis has its antithesis and every argument has its counterargument. That in a way can be kind of disillusioning because you can never come down on either side and say for sure this is it. Everything remains a mystery in a way, ultimately. That's not always so good. As for your question, I guess the "more" is the "more" that is in everyone, straight or gay—all the spiritual and psychological things in people. Sex *is* what makes homosexuals homosexual. Gore Vidal claims there are only homosexual acts, no homosexuals. But in fact, acting in this homosexual way—having sex with a person of the same sex—seems to, at this time and place at least, influence one's life in so many other ways. (That's obvious.) What I mean is, while sex is what makes us homosexual, it is also the thing around which our deep wishes coalesce: the desire for love, trust, fidelity, stability, a home, a companion, a future, all of that. It is *this* aspect of homosexuality I don't think homosexuals have dealt with yet. Can—or how do homosexuals make a home for themselves and each other, give themselves shelter?

CS: In *Nights in Aruba,* Vittorio says at one point that he is jealous of lesbians and that it was the only solution [212]. What does he mean by that? Is that related to the observation that lesbians in your books always seem to appear in a happy twosome, living together, while gays tend to run after a love that, once found, they can't bear to live with?

AH: The image of lesbians is that they *do* make a home with one another, more often than gay men do. This may be a myth, I don't know. Now lesbians are experimenting with sex along anonymous gay male lines, or at least when I did an article on the baths recently for a magazine, I had to interview a woman in San Francisco who runs a lesbian sex club and who says she would like to open a bathhouse for women. That women too want to be able to have public sex, et cetera. This startles people who do not think women's sexuality is as important to them as it is to men. I have no way of knowing if it is, or rather, if women *do* think of sex differently than men. Most people would say they do. Lesbians have this image of forming pairs for longer periods, of not looking for sex in parks, toilets, et cetera, as gay men do, of therefore somehow being "superior"—happier, more intimate, domestic, personal. This may all be a *complete* myth; I'm sure it is in part. But I just talked to a lesbian in Florida who has a monogamous relationship with a woman she has been with for eleven years, and talking to her, I felt this gap between my life and hers—gay women and gay men—though obviously I know several gay male couples who have been together for a long time. . . . This all gets back to how sexuality is expressed differently in men and women, period, not just gay men and women, don't you think? Are men questers, more romantic, than women? Is it Odysseus versus Penelope? I don't know.

CS: A question about politics: You say that the liberation of homosexuals in the seventies had largely expressed itself as promiscuity and less in political action, because homosexuality is about sex, and sex is private [*Ground Zero*: 197]. I disagree; sex is not private. The sexual act may occur in privacy but always within a social system, with certain rules and codes. Different sexual practices have different social and political meanings. The private sex of homosexuals is the basis for their social exclusion and what they in turn used for their political statement—at least for gays. Gay and lesbian sexuality seems to be regarded differently by societies; historically, male homosexuality has been considered more threatening. And so forth. That sex is private is—

to me—just another social construction produced for good reasons.

AH: I think this gets into Foucault, whom I haven't read that much of, and the essentialist versus constructivist debate: Is the homosexuality we practice now a function of our times, cultures, et cetera? Of course. Yet I can conceive of a homosexual man leading a *very* homosexual life and having *nothing* to do with gay life or politics. In fact, like the paradox that people in health food stores always look ill, I have often thought the more political a gay person, the *less* interesting his private or sex life. Sex *is* private and personal, and a person can be richly homosexual without ever taking part in gay politics. The argument, of course, is that the political filters down to influence even that person somehow. But while I believe this for a lot of people, I am always being surprised, especially in Florida, out of the city—where gay styles, politics, mores seem to originate—by people leading homosexual lives, or lives that include a same-sex partner, in otherwise nonhomosexual milieus.

CS: In your essays you say: "Sex is in a sense an exam one takes over and over again" [168]; you also talk about "learning sex" through tricking [149f.]. It reminded me of Jane Rule's comment: "Sex is not so much an identity as a language which we have for so long been forbidden to speak that most of us learn only the crudest of its vocabulary and grammar" [*Outlander*: 185]. What both statements have in common, it seems to me, is an emphasis on the fact that we have very little in terms of sex education. There is too much taboo on sex. What do you think?

AH: They always say Europe has less teen pregnancy, et cetera, than America because we are puritanical and prudish about sex and refuse to allow sex education. But how can one learn sex except by doing it? That's a silly question; of course one can learn from books and teachers, so I am in favor of sex education, yes. What I meant by that line in the essay is more pessimistic—it's that gay men "rate" each other sexually, try each other out, over and over, and measure their partners against essentially pornographic standards and never even reach perhaps a level of intimacy, honesty, consideration, where certain kinds of sex can occur. That's what the phrase "fast-food sex" is all about. Fast food is junk. Junk sex—though anonymous sex can be extremely thrilling, deep, satisfying. Sex is an audition, a test one takes over and over again because one is always meeting, or failing to meet, a new partner's expectations, fantasies, et cetera.

CS: From your novels I got the impression that there is a split between the city and the country. Life in the city means hope and dissatisfaction, and life in the country means peace and dissatisfaction. [*Holleran laughs heartily.*] If you are in the city, there is selfishness; in the country there's family. And Paul, this character in *Nights in Aruba,* says he only feels at peace when he is in transit, when he's in between these two places. Can you comment on that?

AH: You've commented on it right there. I think there is a kind of split there, and it's certainly reflected in my own life, and that's why I wrote about it. And that the physical separation of the family and gay life probably reflects a split in my own conception that isn't resolved. But now, though I've been living in the country for quite a few years and I've had to make a gay life there, I've been struck by the fact that all gay culture—or if you want, gay movement—is from the cities. It is exclusively urban. Everything that has happened has come out of the cities, not the countryside; and that countryside, which I romanticized in a way, is pretty awful in many ways for gay people.

CS: And family and city don't go together at all?

AH: Not in my own personal experience. But I think that was characteristic of most of the gay people I knew in New York. I used to think that everyone was detached from his family. That's why they'd gone to the city. Very few people I knew lived with their families in New York. I can't think of any . . .

CS: What is family?

AH: Okay. I know what you're saying now. I mean family in the sense of parents and relatives. The family out of which we're produced. And now, of course, the trendy thing—say on television, with sit-coms, *Golden Girls* and everything—is that we do not need this traditional nuclear family. That we construct ourselves out of whoever we consider our family. And that's true. Our friends are our family. Absolutely. Very much for gay people. I finally found very good friends in the country in Florida, and they mean an enormous amount to me and are my family. Absolutely.

CS: For me, the city used to mean pollution and noise. That hasn't changed, but now I see the country is really no unpolluted paradise either. In your essays you describe your perplexity and disgust at your discovery that even homosexuals litter. What is your view of the ecological situation worldwide?

AH: I am such an ecologist that I think people who litter should be electrocuted! I can't stand what we have done to the seas. I think the green movement is absolutely a substitute for religious energy and is going to be more and more important. And since overpopulation is at the root of all this, I wonder if homosexuality isn't a "solution," as some people argue. On the other hand, I think there are so many paradoxes the public isn't aware of in this matter—what really damages the environment and what does not.

CS: Do you think you're a city writer, a New York writer? You wrote wonderfully about Florida and the island.

AH: But I love New York very much still. I will always want to write about it. It's hard when you're out of New York because you're not in touch with what New York is now. New York is constantly changing. And if I wrote about it, I would have to write not about the immediacy of New York as I was able to in the past.

CS: I thought you had an amazing talent to describe noises and smells and colors.

AH: Thanks. I love to do that. I love to describe. If you could only write books of descriptions, I would. And that's what I'm trying to do in this book now, that's set in Florida. I'm trying to describe Florida in a more comprehensive way. But you've got to have plots. You've got to have stories to go with the description, and that's what's harder.

CS: In *Dancer from the Dance,* especially, I got the impression that the relationship between different ethnicities wasn't so much a problem as in the society at large. You describe that when you say in New York one is in love with Italians and Jews and so forth. Did living in New York help develop something like a bi- or pluricultural consciousness?

AH: Because I grew up on a Dutch island, with Caribbean people and American and European, I have never had a problem with pluricultural life, I guess, and I always loved New York City from the beginning because of its different groups. But I had this in me before I went there I think. I *was* thinking that the relationship between different ethnicities wasn't so much a problem as in the rest of society. And in actual fact, now it's a tremendous problem. This ethnicity has become such a problem, and reading that book there's a tremendous freedom. It's an aesthetic freedom. Tonight you can have a Puerto Rican. Tomorrow you can have an Italian. Then you can have . . . It's like a wonderful appreciation of the differences, and I don't think that's changed. If you're gay in New York, that's the kind of freedom that still is there.

CS: But that is only within the gay community?

AH: Yes, but that was the paradox of the gay community. It broke down all the barriers because being gay means you're outcast. It's what you have in common, and all the social things fall away so that there was an amazing mixture and there still is I'm sure.

CS: Also blacks? You didn't mention them.

AH: No. Black gay men have started their own magazines now, they're starting their own anthologies now, and they're claiming that nothing reflects them except their own writers and their own magazines. So yes, I think that the black/white segregation did exist, more than any other segregation. On the other hand, I don't think there was nearly the nervousness when a black gay person came anywhere in New York that I was at that there would have been in another situation. I think that the gay democracy and the breakdown of the social classes existed for blacks too. But for some reason the black/white segregation still pertained. There was a bathhouse in New York called "Man's Country," which they tried to start out as a popular "white" bathhouse. It became black and Puerto Rican, and then it shifted entirely to black and Puerto Rican. And I kept going there because I liked it very much, but no one I knew went there, and there were more examples of things tipping. It's very hard to find a balance, to find integration. It would tip one way or another. So it is a problem that existed even in gay life.

And blacks have had a terrible time of it. There was an essay in the *New Republic* by Andrew Sullivan about AIDS in the black community, about how the black churches would not even mention the word. Black politicians would not even mention the word because homosexuality was even more of a taboo in the congregations and in the churches than it was anywhere else. And yet the problem was getting worse and worse. It took a while before gay politicians in Congress or the ministers would even talk about it. So gay men have suffered homophobia in black society in addition to oppression by white society—which is ironic because Americans' stereotype of blacks is that they're sexually freer, more relaxed. But that's not true, at least in the sense of homophobia.

CS: Where do you situate yourself as a writer? Do you mainly feel that you belong to a certain group in the States, or do you think you're a typical American writer? Do you consider yourself "mainstream," "experimental," "gay"?

AH: I can't answer it because I'm very surprised that all of this has turned out the way it has. In the end I wrote the first book because I just took a chance in writing that material. It turned out that was a successful book, and it put me in a category that I've stayed in. I know there have been people all along who have said, "Won't you write a cross-over book?" A cross-over book is considered a gay book that is popular with mainstream audiences too. Or there are even examples of gay writers who have taken nongay topics, but I can't imagine tailoring a book to an audience or to your career. I think that would be crazy.

CS: So you don't have a certain audience in mind when you write? You don't write for gay people?

AH: No . . . I do, though. As a matter of fact I do because I write about gay things. Why do I write about gay things? Because obviously my gayness obsesses me. And why does it obsess me? I don't know, but writing about it is a way to deal with that obsession. At this point in my life I do ask myself, why have I been obsessed with my whole sexuality? Because obviously there are other men who are gay or women who are gay, who have gay lives, gay personal lives, and think of themselves in other terms—of their career, as doctors, as scientists or whatever. I don't know why in my case it merged with the writing.

CS: Have you experienced discrimination in publishing or in daily life?

AH: No discrimination in publishing at all. In daily life, I can't think of any, except the fact that I have restricted myself in many ways, I'm sure, because of my gayness. In other words, one lives and goes places where it won't be a problem, the fact that one is gay.

CS: What are your connections to Germany, to Europe?

AH: I romanticize Europe and Germany, I think, partly because my father's family is all of German-American stock and partly because I love the arts and culture. And partly because I am not European, I guess. I was very happy in the year I was in Heidelberg, and I am happy on this visit. I loved Berlin, but my German friend who lives there wants to get out . . .

CS: What is the role of the writer?

AH: The role of the writer is nothing more than to write as well as he can about what is beautiful or important or moving to him. To be as honest as possible. To give pleasure. To convey how he or she sees the world.

CS: Has gay writing come to where being gay is no longer its main concern but one fact among others? I am asking also because sometimes I saw a glimpse of that in your essays, like when you write about AIDS and dying. Being gay in that context is really an accident. The real problem there is how to deal with death.

AH: From the time my first novel was published, I met gay people who would say, "Can't you write a book in which being gay is just a minor part of the story?" But this always seemed to me a bit deluded. If one writes well, even if being gay is a *big* part of the story, it will still be about dying, aging, trying to love, et cetera. As gay books come out more and more, however, I do think writers are being forced to expand their subject matter, because one can only write a coming-out story or a gay-acceptance-of-identity story once, or twice. I find this problem now with my next book; I don't want to repeat myself. (Yet of course I will, in some way.) There are gay critics who complain that most gay books now are as banal and middle-class and mainstream as any other sort of book. They call this "dickless" lit, that is, literature without a penis. But gay writing, as a subspecies, has to evolve.

CS: Do you consider yourself an idealist?

AH: Yes, though I'm not sure what this means anymore. The question might be, in what way are you an idealist?

THREE

ALAN LELCHUK

interviewed by
Regine Rosenthal

Alan Lelchuk was born in Brooklyn, New York, in 1938. He was educated at Brooklyn College and Stanford University, where he received a doctorate in 1965, and spent a year abroad at the University of London. He began writing short stories and articles of literary criticism for such journals as The Atlantic Monthly, *the* New American Review, *the* New Republic, Partisan Review, New York Times Book Review, *and* Sewanee Review. *Joining Philip Rahv, he helped found the influential literary journal* Modern Occasions *in 1970.*

His career as a novelist began in 1973 with the publication of American Mischief. Miriam at Thirty-Four *appeared in 1975, and its sequel,* Miriam in Her Forties, *in 1985. His novel* Shrinking *(1978) was honored as one of the "best novels of the year" by the* New York Times. *In 1987* On Home Ground, *for young adults, was published, and* Brooklyn Boy *appeared in 1990. His new novel,* Playing the Game, *will be out in the spring of 1995.*

As one of the best-known contemporary Jewish-American authors, Lelchuk has received numerous honors, among them a Guggenheim Fellowship. His dramatic presentation of artistic, political, and sexual problems has earned him much praise but has also placed the author at the center of heated debates in intellectual circles. Alan Lelchuk has taught at Brandeis, Amherst, and CCNY, and since 1985 has been on the faculty of the Liberal Arts Graduate Program at Dartmouth College.

RR: I would like to start with a few biographical data or questions. As you mention in your texts, your father grew up in Russia and later emigrated to the States, so you could be called second-generation immigrant Jew. Did this Russian past of your father's—and I don't know anything about your mother—play any role in your own growing up in the United States? In other words, did he pass on to you an idea of America and its values which you wanted to emulate, or had he grown disenchanted with what he found? Maybe you could tell us something about the part of your mother, too.

AL: What my father wanted to pass on to me was not what I received and not what I grew up with. My father wanted to pass on to me his values about Russia, about communism, and about his motherland and his adverse opinions about America and capitalism; well, naturally, I wound up developing the opposite opinions and values. I had little interest in Russia or in Bolshevism, but I had great interest in all things American and grew up *determinedly* American. Baseball is a classic example, a kind of metaphor for my Americanness. About things Jewish it was more complicated, because he was both a Communist and a Zionist, a convenient contradiction. I did not grow up being either a Communist or a Zionist; but he did teach me Hebrew for my bar mitzvah and he did send me to a first-class Socialist-sponsored Bund school, which emphasized a Yiddish education, and I quite liked it—for five years or so. And that Sholom Aleichem School was a value and was his doing. There I learned how to read and write Yiddish and received a pretty good introduction to Yiddish literature, because the *Lehrer,* or teacher, happened to be—I didn't know this then—a serious Yiddish poet, who published three books of real poetry. Anyway, from age eight to thirteen or so, we read stories written for children by Yiddish masters like Peretz and Mendele, the Singer brothers, and so on. And we read Jewish history via the Bible, and even though a Bund school was a Socialist school, it was a completely apolitical education. Yet, as I've said, it was very Yiddish-oriented, so my grounding in things Jewish was by means of Yiddish, both from the school and from home, where my parents spoke Yiddish half the time, especially if they wished to say something private.

Anyway, my father's values were very Russian, authoritarian values, and those qualities were rejected by me; and that rejection caused great difficulty between us, starting at the age of seven or eight. So my values were developed half through rejection, opposition. Yet I opposed him not really because of things Russian or Communist; I opposed him because of his difficult personality, the way he dealt with my mother, and the way he started dealing with me. So that's why I rejected the other things I might otherwise have been more tolerant of. Here's a nice little story: When I was one year old, my father bought tickets for us to go back to Russia, ostensibly for a vacation, and we were already on the ship when my sister developed a bad earache. The doctor came and said, "You have a bad infection, you must go to the hospital." My father said, "No, no, we'll deal with it on the ship," but my mother said, "No, we're not crossing the ocean with her having an infection." So we put her in the hospital. And that week Germany invaded Poland, and we never went to Russia and I never grew up Russian—because of my sister's earache. So I have my sister's earache to thank for my growing up an American boy. A nice stroke of luck, wouldn't you say?

RR: So your father didn't have the foresight to see the political situation in Europe and not to go back?

AL: He wanted to go; he wanted to go back and stay there. His dream was to return to Russia and to return to his family. He didn't like America; he never understood it, and he felt strange, out of place, a permanent foreigner.

RR: And you, as the second generation, you wanted to assimilate, and you wanted to be part of America in strong opposition to the first generation?

AL: Yes, but again, opposition to this particular father was the crucial matter. And I never felt assimilation into America was as simple as either turning the radio on or taking a walk. My father was not a religious Jew, but he did ridiculous European things with me that the other fathers wouldn't dream of. He would dress me up in woolen knicker suits. You remember those? Complete with a tweed cap. And the kids would laugh and mock me like crazy. I'd wear these high woolen stockings, with the cap, and look like a greenhorn, or newcomer.

RR: Very embarrassing for you.

AL: It was very embarrassing, and everyone laughed and ridiculed. Then on Sundays he would insist that we go uptown to Manhattan to see Russian movies only—in Russian—maybe also Charlie Chaplin, in the famous Stanley Theater on Fourteenth Street, a hotbed for Russian exiles. And I had to wear those knicker suits to go uptown, and it was a real ordeal. Yet paradoxically there was also a part of it that I looked forward to, the ritual of Sundays alone with father, that I couldn't quite explain to myself, though later I understood it better, when I wrote "Sundays," a section of *Brooklyn Boy.*

RR: And you could speak Russian, you could understand the movies?

AL: As a very little boy I spoke and understood a little Russian. I would emphasize *understood* Russian, rather than spoke it. Soon enough, my mother insisted that he stop speaking to me in Russian, just in case.

RR: She wanted you to be integrated.

AL: She wanted me to be American and that he should have little or no influence with Russian over me. And so she got him to stop speaking Russian to me and to speak only English to me. My mother was not from Russia, you see; she was born in America. But she was not really very American; she was not exactly an immigrant, but at times perhaps she acted like one.

RR: And her parents were not immigrants?

AL: Yes, they were from Russia. She was an immigrant's daughter.

RR: But then she knew better about your problems than your father did.

AL: That's right.

RR: She could . . .

AL: . . . negotiate them better and therefore insisted that I grow up American.

RR: So in other words, Jewishness as such did not play such a big role for you. You didn't go to synagogue or . . .

AL: We went to the synagogue on occasion, but we didn't go in a religious way. Jewishness played an important role, but it was a cultural kind of Jewishness. For example, I went to that Bund school for five years, every afternoon after regular public school. The Sholom Aleichem school was a decidedly secular school. The idea of the school was to maintain and to spread Yiddish culture for children growing up in America, for the immigrants' kids. Literature, history, even games and Jewish humor. Later on, I did a bar mitzvah in Hebrew with my father—not a rabbi—and remember, too, my parents spoke Yiddish in the household. If it was a high holiday, like Rosh Hashanah or Yom Kippur, I went to the shul, or synagogue, which was two blocks away. So I grew up, you see, immersed in Jewishness, but it was not religious but cultural and secular.

RR: So did you grow up in a bicultural consciousness? Did you have the feeling of a double identity—Jewish and American—that you had to negotiate somehow?

AL: Yes, absolutely. But it was not a difficult negotiation because I grew up in a fundamentally Jewish neighborhood, with maybe half the kids sons and daughters of immigrants. Yet the neighborhood was definitely American—the language and schools, the movie houses and the sports, the aspirations and dreams. We looked ahead, not back.

RR: You kids all had the same problems?

AL: Well, they didn't have quite the extreme situation I did because none of them had a father who was such an odd man out, such an unreconstructed Russian Bolshevik. They were solid shopkeepers and merchants, and he was more intellectual and more European-formal. But the two identities for me did not have any conflict essentially then. There were small things, small immigrant habits, such as the kind of food that he made at home. My father would cook frequently and reproduce his East European tastes, such as *Plate flanken,* or boiled beef, heavily salted and overcooked, like everything else, and it was dreadful. And there would be growing conflict when I no longer would wear those knicker suits or want to eat his kind of food, and those protests or rebellions made things very difficult.

RR: What is your definition of Jewish-American literature or of a Jewish-American writer? Would you define him/her as somebody who happens to be born a Jew or as somebody who deals with the problems of being Jewish in America?

AL: The more interesting point for me is someone who demonstrates or manifests Jewishness in the text but not Jewishness by the actual content of going to a shul, lighting candles on a Friday night, reciting the Hebrew prayers, and so on. That's Jewish content, yes, but not necessarily interesting for literature. To me it's more interesting how it reveals itself in the text. For example, I think that Grace Paley is not particularly interested in, say, things Jewish, but the rhythms in her language and the unusual perspective strike me as very Jewish. Whereas Bellow, for example, he writes about Jewish intellectuals, yes; but also the essentials of his work, the rhythms of the prose, the inflections and the Yiddishisms, the tremendous sense of irony—all that I connect up with the most potent aspects of Jewishness in American writing and literature. And I think in my books—in the Miriam novels, in *American Mischief* and *Shrinking*—Jewishness manifests itself in the textures of the narratives, the humor, the irony, the intense or overwrought sensibility of the narrators. Those strike me as more Jewish-American than any traditional or conventional Jewish rituals. So that's how I perceive it. And that's why a "conventional" Jewish content in novels doesn't particularly interest me.

RR: You have to feel the tension.

AL: Right. There are tensions and ambivalences in the text that have much less to do with conventional notions of Jewish writing and Jewishness. Bellow is the best example of it, but you also see those tensions in Roth, for example, or in Paley's stories.

RR: How do you feel about the term *ethnicity*? Do you reject it, as Cynthia Ozick does, as a "debased or debasing sociologist's misnomer," or do you accept the term "ethnic writer" for yourself? Do you like to be labeled an ethnic writer?

AL: Well, I once gave a talk precisely on this subject for the University of Massachusetts Humanities Institute. And I said then—and I still feel—that ethnicity as a badge of honor is not a badge that interests me but that the strong Jewish element which has existed in my life is a strong component of the fiction and emerges in a more sophisticated way, as ethnic material converted into literature, I hope. So I don't look upon myself as an ethnic writer; I think of myself as an American writer for whom Jewishness has been a crucial component.

RR: So you don't have a problem with the term *ethnic*?

AL: I don't have a problem with it, but I wouldn't put the label on myself. If someone calls me an ethnic writer, that's his prerogative. In the old days it was a derogatory term; nowadays it's a kind of laudatory term, but for me it doesn't hold much interest.

RR: What is your idea of the term *multiculturalism,* a term that has been widely used and abused recently and seems to have replaced the term *ethnicity*?

AL: I feel that it has opened the doors and the windows of classrooms to more accessibility, to many more ways of seeing things and hearing different voices, and all that's to the good. But there's been a downside to it, too, and that is the inflation of many of these texts so that what is studied are frequently *sub*literary forms. Those texts are not yet up to the standards of true literature, as I perceive it, and that's because it's an era of transition right now for many of these more marginal voices and cultures. I would imagine that in the next ten years or so, we'll see a higher level or more developed literary line. Just now, however, many of these texts are in American university life for political reasons, not literary ones. Certainly, if I were a certain kind of writer from what may be called—and I don't like to call it that—a minority culture—and I don't feel myself as a part of a minority culture at all, as a minority writer—I would call the term tautological. But if I thought that multiculturalism opened up doors to getting published, then I think it's useful. And in certain curriculums across the country perhaps it's been useful. Yet in many curriculums important American writers have been edged aside for the sake of misguided democratic and political reasons, not for literary reasons. An American student needs to know Melville, Hawthorne, Twain, Wharton, Crane as the *basis* for his or her knowledge of the native literature. Race and gender are less significant than excellence here. So I think it has had a two-sided effect for education. As for literary people, it strikes me as a kind of pseudo-issue, for the most part. Different voices, different writers, have always been read and appreciated by the literary world. Difference itself has always been a reason for celebration, be it style or content, *if* there's a literary quality to it. What is literature, if not an original voice, a newly gained territory, a different perspective on the familiar?

Let me make one further point. For years the Jewish writer fought hard for his place on the stage of American literature and finally won it on the basis of his achievement. (That moment arrived in 1954, when Bellow won the National Book Award for *Adventures of Augie March*; soon thereafter, Katherine Anne Porter lamented the giving of the award to Bellow, saying that it encouraged corruptions in the language.) Now with multiculturalism, the position of the Jewish writer is perhaps once again thrown into some question. Is he or she to be considered a minority writer, a status and label that he has sought to overcome in the past? Or is he considered a part of that establishment elite and status quo that has been responsible at times for resisting new voices and new works? Once again the Jewish writer may be burdened with an odd role, that of insider and outsider at the same time.

RR: What is your relationship to Israel? You have twice quite extensively lectured and taught in Israel, could you ever imagine yourself making *aliya,* or do you feel too much of an American to emigrate to Israel?

AL: I feel much more American than I feel Israeli, and even if I had thought about *aliya,* which I don't, it'd be very hard for me to be serious about it because of the language—you know I write in English, and my subject is America and American protagonists, even though one of the new things that I'm writing has to do with an American who goes to Israel, comes and goes, goes back and forth. But I have warm feelings about Israel even though I've resented strongly the ongoing situation of occupation and the politics of the right wing. A lot of people forget, however, that the politics of the Right has existed everywhere in the world in the last fifteen years—Thatcherism in England, Reaganism in America, Kohl in Germany, and so on. So Israel too has had a right-wing conservative regime, and happily it has just ended; I think there'll be brighter times for Israel. But on the whole I think it's a country that has done very well for forty-four years of existence under a lot of pressures, tremendous pressures and constant hostilities, and I find it most depressing that in the culture of the Left—of which I was a part—anti-Israeli feeling and Israeli bashing have become a common denominator. And sometimes anti-Israeli bashing comes with antisemitic undertones, with both old Leftists and new, causing a good number, like myself, to feel disturbed and disaffected. Across the campuses in America, it's been a most unseemly sight to see the way anti-Israeli feeling has been a part of a convenient conspiracy, grouping America, Israel, and other democratic nations—those two principally—with South Africa. It's been a vulgar categorizing of the cheapest and most cunning sort, and it has included antisemitic traits.

But my own sentiments are very strong about Israel as a developing democracy and as an intensely exciting place, something like New York was thirty years ago. You know how Jerusalem and Tel Aviv are—people from all places come there to mix, to fight, to argue. My, can they argue! So it's a very different place from the headline views of Israel, which deal mainly with political items that are often convenient to the Christian West, especially the Christian anti-Israeli West.

RR: Brandeis University was founded after World War II by Jews to open up the academy also to Jews, to offer equal opportunity to those who had suffered under widespread antisemitism in America and at the universities before the war. Had your decision to teach at Brandeis for so many years anything to do with this fact?

AL: Let me just straighten out a few facts. Brandeis was opened in 1948 because the Jewish community wanted to have one liberal arts college for American students of all faiths, although predominantly Jewish, with a Jewish sponsorship. It was not to be a religious school; they had Yeshiva University. So its idea was to have a great university with a Jewish denomination, in the same way that Harvard or Yale was a great university with a Christian denomination sponsoring it. In the first twenty-five years or so it was a very exciting university, and professors left other places to come to Brandeis. And I came to Brandeis for several reasons. I was on the West Coast, getting a Ph.D. at Stanford when Irving Howe had just come, having left Brandeis, and he recommended it to me, saying it was still an exciting place, with people like the poet J. V. Cunningham and the critic Philip Rahv, among others. So, too, the atmosphere of Jewish excitement was still there, because some of the great critics of America were there, like Herbert Marcuse, the psychologist Abraham Maslow, the historian Frank Manuel, and Leo Bronstein, a well-known art historian. Altogether there were about half a dozen nationally known intellectuals who made the faculty an inspiring arena. As to whether I went because it was Jewish: if it were Jewish and mediocre, I wouldn't have gone, but since it was Jewish and exciting, it interested me. Also, the undergraduates were first-class, an important point.

RR: Could you please tell me something about the shaping influence Philip Rahv had on you? Rahv, the powerful literary critic and long-time editor of the very influential leftist journal *Partisan Review* and editor of *Modern Occasions,* a journal you worked on together with him.

AL: Well, Rahv was, to my mind, a great literary historian and a formidable critic. I wrote a piece in memory of him, which perhaps you've seen. While he was especially a great critic of Russian literature, he was also one on American literature. And remember, Rahv's first language was Yiddish; his second, Russian, and his *third language,* English. Only at eighteen or nineteen he learned English. So his development into a first-rate stylist was quite an amazing feat. Anyway Philip, when I first came to Brandeis in 1966, took me under his wing, figuratively and literally. I remember meeting him for the first time at a party, and he took my arm in his and went *spazieren* around the rooms, strolling around and linking my arm in a way that was completely foreign to me and not an American way of doing things. I was most flattered. After all, I was nobody, a fresh assistant professor on campus, while Rahv was one of the four or five most well-respected literary critics in America at the time. Trilling and Wilson and a few others, maybe Howe, and a few from the Southern school—Tate, Jarrell—but they all looked up to Rahv theoretically.

Almost immediately he provided a kind of Oxford personal tutorial for me, Russian-Jewish style, a serious education. He gave me things to read, like Herzen's *Memoirs,* that I had never read before, introduced me to writers like Leskov and Bunin, talked to me about books and politics steadily for ten, fifteen years, you realize. . . . Books and left-wing politics—well, women and gossip, too; that also was his interest. And in the beginning years I took a lot of what he was saying in a kind of uncritical way, but gradually, you know, I began to see that I had different views from him about things, political and personal things. But he was certainly one of the formidable influences of my literary career; and when I finished *American Mischief,* my first book, he read the whole thing in manuscript, along with Philip Roth, and was one of my major benefactors. He wanted to publish a section of it, in fact, in *Modern Occasions,* the section about Mailer, but was dissuaded from it by his friend Robert Silvers of the *New York Review of Books,* who said Mailer will sue you so bad, the magazine will go bankrupt. So he held off and didn't publish it; but he was one of my two main readers *and critics* of the manuscript—Rahv and Philip Roth. So Rahv was a combination of father figure and literary mentor, a literary father essentially. In later years, he proved to be a very difficult man. Finally, I sort of had to break off from him entirely, and it was too bad, though just before his death we had a reconciliation.

I'll just add one last thing: In the recent memoir by Sidney Hook, about the forties and fifties—and this was pointed out to me by Saul Bellow, a dear mutual friend of Philip's and mine—Hook makes a very damning criticism about Rahv, saying he was a one-dimensional Bolshevik and so on, but this view completely misunderstood Rahv. His politics were one thing, but he had a whole literary side wherein he loved books, loved literature, and was one of its best friends and critics. They don't make his mold any more. Roth, Bellow, Sartre, McCarthy, among many, sent us something for *Modern Occasions,* for hardly any pay; that's what Rahv's name meant. He taught me what serious editing was.

RR: You just mentioned Philip Roth. He gave a favorable criticism of your first book, so he too was kind of starting you in your literary career. Are you still in touch with him?

AL: Yes, I saw Philip about ten days ago. We had a very good time. Roth was very important to the making of *American Mischief* because I was working on a different book when I met him at Yaddo, an artist colony in upstate New York, and we became fast friends; and it was he who read forty pages of manuscript, which was to become *American Mischief.* And he told me to put down what I was writing and work on this manuscript instead. But I couldn't do it. So he then told me the story of how in Chicago he was working on a novel as a graduate student and told his friend, Richard Stern, over beers, about another story. And Stern said, "Put down what you're writing and write this story." And he insisted, and Roth acquiesced and wrote the story, and it became "Goodbye, Columbus." So when I heard that, I felt more convinced to put my long manuscript down and instead, for the next four years, worked on *American Mischief.* I even gave back money which I had from a publisher, Houghton Mifflin, as an advance on the other book. I just worked steadily on *American Mischief,* really through Philip's encouragement and criticism too. He would read the manuscript as I worked on it; in other words I'd write fifty pages or so and show it to him. So he was a very important influence as critic and friend.

RR: Was there an influence of Bellow in your fiction? You mention Augie March, the protagonist of Bellow's 1953 novel *The Adventures of Augie March,* in your story "Adventures of a Fiction Boy."

AL: Bellow is and was to me the great writer of our time. I first read his books underground, when I was sixteen and the fiction boy in Schulte's Fourth Avenue Book Store, as my story talks about. He was a great influence in the sense of loving to read his novels and admiring his vast talent. You couldn't emulate Bellow's style. I mean I didn't wish to because I think he is a great, great stylist, but his risk-taking and his integrity and his freedom as a writer and his material, of course—a certain kind of tormented, humorous, self-ironic Jewish hero—appealed to me tremendously, even though Bellow himself was twenty-five years older than I am, approximately. The material appealed to me like no other material, the mix of the high and the low, the intellectual and the ludicrous, the Jewish and the Gentile. I got to know Bellow when I was a graduate student at Stanford and he came to give a talk. I wrote him a note and said I was "an aspiring writer, and graduate student here, would you like to have a coffee or a walk?" And indeed he called me and said, "Yes, let's have a coffee and a walk," and that's how I met him. And we stayed friends, very good friends, for the last thirty years. Of course, he knew Rahv well and knew Roth and was friends with both of them.

If you know him well, Bellow is a great man. He can be, with a lot of people, a very difficult man, a quirky man, an eccentric man, but he's a great literary figure who loves books and talks about them most intelligently. You know, the thing about Roth and Bellow and Rahv that you just can't get every day is that they love books and talk about books, and they don't obfuscate it with theories or taint it with foolish politics. They talk about what's good and what's bad and *why* in a book, and *not* about agents or publishers, that sort of drivel. In other words, it's been a true inspiration to have a great literary figure on the scene for nearly fifty years, writing novels and stories and essays about the role of literature. You see, in our world, which has been so corrupted by money and celebrityhood and nonliterary distraction, to have somebody who has remained a pure literary soul is kind of remarkable.

RR: Many critics have found fault with your open and daring treatment of sex in your first books, especially *American Mischief* and *Miriam at Thirty-Four.* Many have even attacked it as pornography. What was your reason for going so far? Could it be that you enjoyed shocking critics and readers alike, or do you agree with some voices who see *American Mischief* as a companion piece to Saul Bellow's *Mr. Sammler's Planet* and the attack there on everything that is wrong with American society?

AL: One thing to understand is that I come from a different generation than the Bellow-Rahv generation and that for me writing about sexual reality in a more open and frank way is not uncommon. Even those, such as Roth or Updike, who are six years older than myself, they've written about sex in a similar sort of way. (And in the past, of course, we've had Henry Miller.) The fact that I started my career in such an aggressive and open way, I think that was very hard for a lot of people to take who might have understood it better in the third or fourth novel, after a few more staid, conventional novels. But I didn't start out that way. I started out with an unconventional text, which itself was a succès d'estime in the very beginning, at its very birth. And this angered a lot of people, too: that a first novelist should be already borne on the wings of critics like Rahv and Roth and, secondly, that it already was financially successful, when it started out. In point of fact, I think a writer can and should write what he or she feels to be the truth about situations, human relations, whatever it may be; and to me sex in America, in certain respects, frequently replaces the drawing room as society or a place of seeing society. You do not have salons and drawing rooms in America the way you did in nineteenth-century England. What you have is a bedroom, and in the bedroom lots of revelations of character come forth, as they do on the couch of some psychiatrist, which is generally more boring for the art of fiction than scenes of intimacy.

And I've tried to relate sexual scenes to character, to development and portrayal of character. It is true that I certainly did not either put on blinders of a censorious nature or restrain myself for the sake of literary diplomacy and that this offended a great number of virtuous souls. Well, virtue—or being virtuous—doesn't interest me as a writer. I think that my scenes of the erotic are anything but mechanical; they're comical and dramatic and what have you. Pornography is something that's mechanical and predictable and has no connection with human character, while my scenes have everything to do with human character. I like to think that if Ibsen or Strindberg were writing today, in plays or in novels (Strindberg's), to use two examples, that a more open treatment of sexuality would be an obvious pursuit. We're not writing literature in the 1880s or so but a hundred years later, and yet still to this day I'm tarred with the charge by certain critics. In the *New York Times* daily review—of my last novel, *Brooklyn Boy,* for example—the woman who reviews there regularly started out her review with a few paragraphs about "Lelchuk's derogatory treatment of women by means of sexual writing in his past books." Judging from that deliberate and tendentious misreading of my work, I wonder if she's ever really read a novel of mine? Ever read my Miriam novels and seen how scenes of sexuality dramatize her needs, her aspirations, her disappointments, her fullest character? Would anyone of honesty and reasonable openness call that treatment derogatory or pornographic? My God, thank God for the general reader out there who has written me, the female professor from Indiana or the social worker from St. Johns, Newfoundland, or the bookseller from Hanover, who reads the surfaces accurately and feels the depths of Miriam's dilemmas sympathetically. Those are the women readers with whom I test my treatment of sexuality in the novels, not the self-styled critic with the tendentious bias, who can't even describe the surface of the book with accuracy, let alone the depths. And this has happened again and again, in the decade. Honest talk and frank scenes require a reader of intelligence, honesty, openness, and experience. Now how many book reviewers have those credentials, plus taste? Not many. And I won't be intimidated or influenced, for the sake of success in certain quarters like the *Times,* to return to the Victorian age for my perspective and my scenes.

RR: So in other words the publication of these early books earned you the name of "bad boy" or "enfant terrible" just as *Portnoy's Complaint* did for Roth?

AL: Yes. And in fact there are a few reviews that I will show you, by Mark Shechner or Sven Birkerts, say, that discuss that label.

RR: Now what role did Norman Mailer play in your literary career?

AL: Mailer had only one place in my career and that was with the first book.

RR: Yes, that bad scene you had the fight about.

AL: That's right. Mailer sent a telegram to the publisher saying, "I've just read this scene and you must not publish *American Mischief* until we've had a meeting." So he ordained a meeting in which he came with his lawyer, who was also his brother-in-law, and I came with my lawyer and also my second, who was Philip Roth. We sat on the twenty-sixth floor in a Manhattan skyscraper for about four and a half hours; and every time he would accuse me of character slander, I would take out a book of Mailer's and say, "Look, this is what you advocated in this essay about kidnapping Jackie Kennedy, this is what you suggested a writer do about his inhibitions, and I was merely following you and your words. Why, I even paid you two hundred and fifty dollars—you probably don't know it—to quote from your article on the White Hipster, which was of use to my character, and you want to censor me?!" Well, the word *censorship* drove him wild, because here was a man who tried to say that he was fighting for freedom from all censorship, and his lawyer, Charles Rembar, had just written a book about censorship! At the end of four and a half hours he threatened me physically, to meet me in an alley and take me on, if he ever met me sometime. And I said, "You're the fighter, Mr. Mailer, and I'm just the writer." Actually, he didn't look at the moment like he could take anyone on, having been up late for a Johnny Carson show. Something like that.

It was Bob Giroux who saved the book for Roger Strauss. Bob Giroux came up to me and said, "I never knew he was so vituperative. Don't worry. I'll take the book over." Because my editor at the time, Henry Robbins, was so intimidated by Mailer that he backed off, although he had read the whole manuscript several times and never once mentioned cutting the scene! And Roger Strauss, the publisher, was afraid of Mailer, so it was Bob Giroux who said "Don't worry about anything. I'll take the book over." Naturally, I kept the scene in. It was a crucial scene where the protagonist, Lenny Pincus, a middle-class sixties rebel, has to learn to cross the boundaries into a new dangerous territory while transforming himself into a true revolutionary. That's where the murder of a famous character called Norman Mailer, based to some extent upon the real Mailer but invented by me, is very important to the political theme and also to the construction of the plot.

RR: Have you not talked to Mailer again?

AL: I've never seen or talked to Mailer again. Curiously enough, he's been asked every few years what he thinks about Alan Lelchuk and *American Mischief,* and it's one of the few topics that he has nothing to say about. Just a few years ago he gave a talk at the University of Pennsylvania, and someone asked him what he thought of me, and he said, "I don't have anything to say about him or that book." I take the silence as an ultimate flattery.

RR: Did you belong to the student movement of the sixties while you studied at Stanford? Do you feel yourself like a rebel of the sixties? Have you been influenced by Charles Reich's *The Greening of America*?

AL: Not at all by that romantic tract. I was a grad student and critic of the sixties, but I was also a critical rebel of the sixties, and *American Mischief* is a demonstration of both the rebellious side and the critical side of the time. I was certainly involved with the movement in a back-of-the-room way, and Leopold Haimson, a historian, and I used to go up to Berkeley to see the Free Speech movement, and we were also involved with the Stanford anti-Vietnam campus rallies. And I remember going to Ann Arbor for a national conference of students and professors which helped begin the teach-ins around the country. But even that was always, you know, looked upon by me with a certain amount of literary inquiry; that's to say I viewed the happenings as possible scenes to be written about. I was immersed politically, yes, but *American Mischief*, I think, manifests both sides of my critical eye—against an abusive government authority and at the same time against the excesses of the movement. So I felt both ways about it. I certainly was totally against the Vietnam War and Johnson-Nixon-Kissinger; that was easy to be, but I was also growing more skeptical about some of the more radical approaches of the students. I don't think American society is an evil empire or ever was; I think it's had some corrupting evil gentlemen at the top—like Nixon—but in our democratic society we've been protected by our constitutional checks and balances. A lot of the radicals felt one hundred percent sour about America. I didn't; I appreciated America. I think *American Mischief* would have been a much simpler book if I didn't hold both notions simultaneously.

RR: Now, why did you write the sequel to *Miriam at Thirty-Four*, that is, *Miriam in Her Forties*? Was it because you had grown older yourself then by ten years and the development in your heroine should reflect the changes that had taken place in yourself?

AL: Well, I had no conscious intention of writing another Miriam. Through the seventies and eighties I got letters from women asking, "What's happened to Miriam?" That got me thinking about what indeed had happened to Miriam, I think—not my own age—and I started taking notes about her. And just recently, in Jerusalem in the spring, I wrote twenty pages of "Miriam in

Her Fifties," the closing sequel for sure about her. It's nice to have readers ask about her, you see. And what you discover is the pleasure of resuscitating characters you have not killed off but just put to sleep for a while in your imagination. Now you open the drawer and there they are; they have a renewed and different life at an older age, and you know them well, they're good friends. So you have a great head start with the imagined territory, and whenever you have a head start with that territory, it's wonderful. You have less to invent in a way, like Shakespeare using English history that he and his audience knew about. So I know this Miriam, and for me to ask the same question that some of these readers were asking, "What's happened to her? Has she hit fifty yet?" spurred me on to think about that evolution. Also one or two of the original models for Miriam are now in their fifties, so that too adds an element of experience to the imagined mix. In fact that's how *Miriam in Her Forties* came into fictional life, a similar evolution.

Anyway, at one of our gatherings, Grace Paley spoke about how the character Faith "works" for her. Well, I'm not sure that Miriam works for me; I think I work for Miriam. Remember too, Miriam was a source of controversy and interesting ambiguity for women who read her. *At Thirty-four* was the source of a symposium at the University of Pennsylvania, where some women found it to be a very antifeminist book and others argued she was a true feminist model. I think it was Professor Nina Auerbach who defended her as one of the first feminist heroes who had serious work accomplishment and credibility. But in the last ten years or so, the idea of a man writing about women has become forbidden, so to speak. It's off limits and "exploitative." A decade ago there was a favorable review of *Miriam* that was sent in to *Ms.* magazine and was rejected because it had the "wrong" view of it. Glad no one told Tolstoy and Anna, or Hardy and Tess, about such ironclad boundaries. I look forward to getting chastised again.

RR: Being naughty again.

AL: Being naughty again. First in her thirties, then in her forties, now in her fifties. So that's what I look forward to, taking her up again *if* she's next.

RR: Now a totally different question. Obviously, you have come here to Germany to read from and discuss your work. Has there ever been a time in your life when you refused to travel to Germany because of what happened here before and during the war, such as Cynthia Ozick still does? She refuses to come.

AL: Well, when I first published *American Mischief* and it was taken by Rowohlt in '74 or '75, I was asked by someone if I was interested in coming over to Germany. At that time I really felt much more reluctant, more ambivalent, and decided against. I felt more relaxed about it now and more interested in seeing it. Twenty-odd years ago, at the beginning of my career, I didn't think that I should simply run off to Germany because they're publishing my book. Through the years I've met Germans, not German Jews but Gentiles, in America, Europe, Israel, and have felt my way through the experience and feel *here* a kind of extra sense of—well, I don't know what the right word is—but an extra set of antennae for hearing anything about German attitudes toward Jews then or German attitudes toward Jews now. Yesterday, when we went on a tour of Nürnberg, which was principally a medieval historical tour and not geared toward the Nazi era, the young man who directed the tour, a history grad student, was remarkably open and honest, I thought, about anything I asked about Nazis and Jews, and he even brought it up on his own. So I felt more confident that I made the right sort of choice upon accepting this decision to come and in getting a glimpse of what Germany is about now. And what I see is that the new generation is very realistic about their history. They're very open and willing about facing the Nazi past and facing relations with Jews, *in part* because I think they have other problems now, and that's an old problem that they've been grappling with for a long time. I can't see blaming young people in their twenties or thirties for the sins of their parents or grandparents.

You know, being a self-conscious Jew as I am and as I perhaps have become more so in the last ten years, it's extremely interesting to see Germany and the younger generation of Germans in the light of one's own built-in myths and preconceptions. Their open attitude toward their dark side and the responsibility of their parents and teachers in the making of Hitlerism is more impressive than, say, the French perception of its Vichy past. On the other hand, you know, I don't *forget*. One doesn't forget what happened, and one shouldn't forget. I'm happy to have come here, and I've been hosted graciously, and it's been with completely open eyes on both sides; but that doesn't mean *forget* what went on here fifty years ago. When I look at the little monument where there used to be a Jewish synagogue—the one in Nürnberg destroyed by that infamous Nazi Julius Streicher—it's real, it's moving, it's disconcerting.

RR: Now what is your assessment of the problem of antisemitism in the States as compared to the recent development in Europe and in Germany? There is a growing antisemitism here—in Eastern Europe, in Germany, and all over Europe as well. What about the States?

AL: Antisemitism in America has increased, as I told you, because of the recent anti-Israeli feeling, which has allowed a lot of antisemites to come out of the woodwork and join in the anti-Israeli bashing. I also think that because of the tremendous split and hostility between Jesse Jackson and the Jews—not to mention Farrakhan—this has also fomented antisemitism among many blacks. That's too bad. I don't think that antisemitism in the near future is a major problem for Jews in America. I don't know about Europe; I think that Europe's traditions of antisemitism go back a much longer way than America's traditions. Jews have always done very well in America. There have been other groups, like blacks or Hispanics, that have been easier to target than Jews as a whole in America. And also Jews have settled absolutely everywhere in America, in every little nook and cranny, every remote outpost. I think religious tolerance is too deeply woven into the fabric of American life, despite certain fundamentalist preaching; also, the presence of Jews in every walk of life and on both sides of the political spectrum, right and left, has made it highly unlikely in the foreseeable future for antisemitism to play a major role. Now, if a Jew were to try to run for president one day, that would be another matter!

RR: Do you know any German author personally and/or in his work? Do you have any connection, in other words, to the German literary scene?

AL: Not really, with the exception of reading books through the years. A favorite of mine, for example, was the small novel *To an Unknown Hero* by Hans Erich Nossack, which faced the Nazi past in a subtle and powerful way. I was sorry not to have written him a note of appreciation before he died. A splendid little book, but it never sold in America. And I've read Grass and Böll, of course, and admired the Grass of *Tin Drum* and *Cat and Mouse* and the Böll of *Group Portrait with a Lady* and the eccentric sensibility exhibited in the short stories. Also the essays of Hans Magnus Enzensberger. Oh yes, I did have a personal encounter with a German TV director for a week or so back in the seventies, when a crew from Cologne came over to do a long video interview with me concerning *American Mischief*—a serious fellow, very interested in the intellectual ideas of the novel. I never did get to see the interview and the documentary, which was shot in Cambridge and out at Brandeis University.

RR: Where would you situate yourself in the contemporary literary scene? Is there a certain school or movement, national or international, you consider yourself part of, or do you work by yourself?

AL: I couldn't answer that. I would simply say that I'm the son of fathers like Roth and Bellow and to a certain extent Mailer and Miller. As *The New Republic* reviewer observed, I'm certainly cut from the cloth of Jewish-American intellectual sensibility, comic irony. It's rather hard for some critics to understand the combination of the erotic with the intellectual, so they don't know how to place me. The tradition is realism, brought up to date, with intellectuals for protagonists; intellectuals who are exuberant, confused, sensual, vulnerable. Being a son of Bellow and Roth is not so easy when the masters are still living and writing, so I may have to wait twenty years for the good reader to perceive the differences. But differences there are, plenty.

RR: Are there aesthetic concepts concerning style and form, that you would like to realize in your work?

AL: You try to create a form that fits the content of the book, rather than artificially containing the content. *Brooklyn Boy* is a good example of something happening that looks extremely simple on the surface, but if you read it well, you see that it's actually more complicated than merely a nice autobiographical novel. There are fragments of essays, little pieces of memoir, factual pieces about the Brooklyn Bridge, Dutch history, et cetera. There are what appear to be stories. It's a real mix of genres, and if I had tried to fit it into either a totally consecutive fictional tale without these little essays or tried to alter it to be a more conventional telling in one way or another, it would have come out, to my mind, a thinner book. Yet one tries to make that eclectic form as seamless as possible so that you don't *see* the techniques. In one of the reviews, by the critic William Pritchard, he talks about how the form is much more complicated than one would expect or imagine or even see immediately upon looking at *Brooklyn Boy.* I appreciated that close a reading. And in looking at form versus content or form and content in a novel, my aim is to get the underlying harmony of a book without having it disturbed by the external form, that is, not diminished or disturbed but rather enhanced, heightened by the form.

RR: How do you assess the future of the Jewish-American novel? About a decade ago you argued that the end may have come for the Jewish writer as an ethnic entity or, in other words, that the time has come for the modern Jewish writer to become just the writer or *a* writer. Do you today still feel the same?

AL: That's a good question. It's a good question because of what you put in, which is that ten years ago I argued that, and what do I think now? First of all, an interesting writer or a great writer makes up his *own* school. Kafka or Proust is his *own* school. I could not predict the future of Jewish-American writing with the kind of confidence and arrogance that critics like Irving

Howe attempt to predict: that it's all over, Jewish-American writing won't exist and it can't exist because the generation of sons-of-immigrants' experience has ended, et cetera, and *they know why.* Writers are not predictable, like piano keys; and schools may be of interest to critics and what have you, but an individual Jewish sensibility will determine the future of that school of Jewish-American writing.

For me personally, as I was saying earlier, there are several ongoing situations, which lead in different paths. One situation is a book that I started in Jerusalem, called "Here and There," concerning an American like myself who goes back and forth constantly between Israel and America. He goes back like a homing pigeon, with a cultivated instinct, and what it means or how it plays itself out, that takes a novel to figure out. Now, another direction is something else I spoke to you about, the anti-Israel bashing that has led to or opened up strains of antisemitism in the culture of America, which I've felt and registered on campus, in society. So it would not surprise me to see a novel involving that recrudescence of anti-Jewishness which ten years ago I couldn't have predicted or wouldn't have imagined. It disturbs me and stays with me, and let's see what happens in the next few years, both in outer reality and in my own mind and sensibility, whether something comes out of that. As long as there are Jews in an overwhelmingly Christian country, there will exist an outsider or a marginal culture, and there will always be a good rich tension for the right writer to make good use of. I don't see that tension ending; I don't see full assimilation happening. I see a kind of dual identity continuing and, if anything, strengthening in recent years. I've not been any less of an American and I've been more of a Jew in the last ten years than I could have imagined.

And I think in a certain way my childhood has come back to play importantly in my own mind, in conjunction with the changing reality in America and in the world. For example, in the fall of '91 I was visiting writer at CCNY, once the Harvard for New York's Jewish kids, and I discovered there antisemitic writings and announcements on the walls, blatantly there, and it's very confusing, very disturbing. It's something one couldn't have predicted a decade ago, so the future is up for grabs because reality is powerful and dynamic, and the cultural tension and the cultural paradoxes will remain in the near future. And all the dire predictions by the pundits, the kind of critical self-fulfilling prophecies that pass for higher criticism, those seem to me to be in the service of the critic himself or the industry of criticism but not really helping a writer in any way and having little to do with the kinds of books that writers may write. That there'll be novels coming out doesn't mean that they'll all be very good books, but here and there you'll find a good book, an interesting book, which is about the same percentage as you always find about any subject.

RR: Now, do you feel that by the propagation of the term *multiculturalism* the tensions will increase between Jewish and other groups?

AL: I don't know. I think it remains to be seen; I think there's the possibility. I think that in this conference and among these people, I haven't seen any tension. It's been generally a supportive situation for all groups, for all of us. But these are writers, and writers feel a certain fraternal bond among themselves, a kind of protective bond; but when you leave the world of writers—especially a small group of writers over here in a foreign country together on a kind of mission—who knows what someone might feel about the Jewish *other* on the panel. After all they're Christians of one form or another with, you know, one Jewish Jew and one other kind of Jew perhaps. And that's not to be unfair at all to Grace Paley—I feel enormously fond of her—but it's to say I feel very differently about Jewishness than she does. But certainly it is possible what you are saying, and certainly what I'm saying to you is that in the redesigning of the American education programs along the lines of multiculturalism, antisemitism has been one of the unforeseen consequences perhaps: one in the form of used-up white males and the other in the feelings about Israel. And you might ask, "Why and how the latter?" Because the notion of hegemony and American imperialism always includes some line about Israel, which then translates—sometimes—into something more sinister than just Israeli-bashing.

Furthermore, I also think that there's resentment in the American Gentile literary establishment over the successes of Roth, Bellow, and Malamud that still exists today. I mean, I think certain prominent figures today, who would not acknowledge it, feel resentment at the power and influence of the golden days of American-Jewish writers so that even writers are not entirely clean or untainted by the old disease. Remember what I said about Katherine Anne Porter's open resentment at *Herzog* winning the NBA award and complaining about the bastardization of the English language by Bellow. Not many in the community would acknowledge that; but I think that if you read a few of the well-known novels in thc recent past by favored Gentile writers in the literary establishment, you'd see the resentment, if not worse, resurfacing. (Though antisemitism never kept Céline or Dostoevsky from writing great novels.) So I don't think that the Jew and the Jewish writer is going to go away and my thoughts of ten years ago, that he'd just be a writer—I still hope that he's just a writer meaning that he has the power to create scenes not because they're Jewish scenes but because they're powerful scenes, I still believe in that—but he still is and will be painted as some kind of Jewish writer by this society. Multiculturalism can work both ways, and it remains to be seen as to how it plays itself out.

FOUR

GRACE PALEY

interviewed by
Birgit Fromkorth and
Susanne Opfermann

Grace Paley, born in 1922, is originally from New York City, which is also the scene of most of her short stories. Although her oeuvre is small, she is considered one of the outstanding representatives of Jewish literature in America as well as one of the best short story writers since the Second World War. After studying in New York, she has also taught at different New York universities.

Her first collection of short stories, The Little Disturbances of Man: Stories of Men and Women in Love, *was published in 1959. Two further volumes of short stories followed:* Enormous Changes at the Last Minute *in 1974 and* Later the Same Day *in 1985. In 1985, a volume of her poetry was published,* Leaning Forward: Poems. Long Walks and Intimate Talks, *a small volume of stories and poems, came out in 1991.* New and Collected Poems *was published in 1992; and in 1994* The Collected Stories.

Grace Paley has been honored with a series of prestigious prizes and scholarships. The stories of this masterful stylist often deal with personal relationships, particularly among the multiethnic population of New York City. They show Grace Paley as an energetic feminist and a prominent advocate of the American peace movement and of environmental protection, who has also commented on issues of political ethics in several publications.

SO: You said somewhere that the three important things in your life are writing, politics, and your family. Let's start with your family. Could you tell us about your parents?

GP: Well, my parents were Russian Jews. They were Socialists, and they were radical youngsters when they were kids. At one point or another my father has even written about some arrests, but the main one was when he was sent to, say, Arkhangelsk, and he and my mother were exiled. Then the czar had a son. When he had a son, he freed all prisoners who were less than twenty-one years old. My parents immediately, with my grandmother and aunts, came to the United States. They had already gone through a pogrom around that time that had killed my uncle, my grandmother's seventeen-year-old son, so they came very eagerly, anxiously, and finally patriotically to the United States.

SO: Who introduced you to literature? Did everybody in your family share in the story-telling? Would you say your father was the person who introduced you to literature?

GP: Oh, I wouldn't say he introduced me. I mean I wouldn't use that expression. I would just say there was a lot of stuff in the house [*laughs*], that's all. It was assumed that a kid would read. Because my parents read and didn't make an issue of it. There were always a lot of books around. My father learned English very quickly and read immediately. Dickens, I think, in the first year. He also learned Italian the first year he came to the United States because he worked for an Italian photographer. The women in the family all went to work in the shops, the garment industry, and put my father through school, so he became a doctor.

BF: Was the world of learning or literature associated more with your father or with your mother?

GP: Oh, it was associated with my father mostly in that sense. My grandmother did try to teach me Russian poems, so there must have been something there—I never got exactly what it was.

But I would say my father read more, talked more. My mother read a lot, too; my aunts as well but not so deeply. In some ways, if you want to put it that way, some of their lives were sacrificed to the education of my father; and as I've said before, it paid off. He did well; he took care of the family. But I think my mother was always sad that she hadn't gone to school. They had a lot of music in the house, too. And my mother liked music; my father did. So we had very early lots of records, classical music, so we lived naturally in that environment.

SO: You said again and again that you were interested in the lives of women and children, and you focus on them in your stories; although when you began writing, this was considered a boring topic. Did you share this view?

GP: I did. I put off writing about it because I thought, who's going to read this stuff, you know. You realize it was after the Second World War and a lot of the literature was heavily masculine, and you can see why. So coming into that world, into literature in a different way, was sort of embarrassing to me actually. I thought, Jesus, these guys are doing such important things. But I was unequivocally interested and pressed and bugged by the lives around me. It got to me. And so I just said one day, "Well, I'm going to do it. That's all. That's what I'm going to write." So I wrote, but I never thought anything would come of it.

BF: Well, usually when you love literature you read all the great works and you're male-identified.

GP: That's true. Exactly!

BF: So when did you start developing a female-centered perspective?

GP: Well, if I hadn't been so interested, I wouldn't have kept writing. I probably would have been more male-identified. But it was writing in itself, and I'm thinking as I wrote, you know, that really made me a much more female-centered person. People say, "Well, were you a feminist?" Well, I was writing those things in the mid-fifties. I was aware of a lot of things. I mean it's not as if I was so naïve. I was not naïve. I already knew that I couldn't stand Henry Miller, for instance. Goodness, I already knew that there was a literature that was not about me, sexually. And I knew that certain literatures didn't free me. I mean I knew without knowing. I couldn't have written an article about it. And I wouldn't have written an article about it, but, you know, you should know there was a book that came out in 1948. It was by a woman named Ruth Hershberger, who was a poet also. She wrote a book called *Adam's Rib.* I bet you could dig it up someplace. It actually talked about what was coming in the sixties and seventies. All the truth that was written later on vaginal politics and female sexual oppression. She really got it down there. So you get hints before your knowledge really comes together like that.

BF: But especially in the fifties there was all this pressure on women to be feminine, the feminine mystique and everything. Now that was just before your first book of stories appeared. Did they praise you for the wrong thing, like writing on the feminine side of life? That could have happened.

GP: That could have happened except that was one of the things that was already bothering me, that I was already thinking about. Also, the women lead unconventional lives. At that point of my life I was already very distressed about relations between men and women, and it's not that I ever was a careerist; that is, I didn't think to myself, oh, because you're a woman, you're not going to do this and that, because I never really wanted to do anything. [*Laughs.*] I wanted to keep writing. I happened to like doing those things that are in the book, like going to the park. I happen to like those things. I never did any of that out of some literary intention or anything. I did it out of sheer pleasure and duty. I believed the children should have air every afternoon. Things like that, you know. Rigorously I felt about that, but I never was pushed in that—not feminist but feminineness—way. It had no effect on me at all, partly because my parents were very angry with me that I wasn't interested in doing anything professional. They were angry that I didn't finish school, which I didn't. They didn't like any of this stuff that I was about, and they wanted me to get a trade, to get a profession, to make something of myself. And get married also, but they didn't want me especially to go back to the kitchen or anything like that. They wanted me to be able to earn a living. Also they—mother, aunts—had a kind of Socialist puritanism: no makeup; be yourself with soap and water. I was a little like that.

BF: Were you teaching at that time?

GP: No. I didn't have any trade. I was a typist. I worked in offices.

SO: You have this focus on women in your work, but the mother-daughter relationship really doesn't figure all that much. To many other women writers it is of the utmost importance. Why is it not for you?

GP: Well, first of all, my mother died when I was about twenty-one or twenty-two, and I was really brought up in a more extended kind of family than is customary in the States. In my house lived my father, my mother, my grandmother, and when I was very young, two aunts, and finally one aunt. So I had all these women taking care of me. So I never had that terrific focus, you know, that a lot of people do have. My grandmother took care of me, my aunt took care of me. My sister is fourteen years older than me, and I think actually she sort of stole me from my mother. I'm not exactly sure; but from the minute I was born, I was in her charge and not because my mother handed me over. But I also had terrible quarrels with my mother when I was in my teens, my adolescence, which were just being resolved really. None of them were because there was anything wrong with her. She was really a remarkable and kind, really a good person, and admired. But she was very puritanical, and this is very hard on teenagers. [*Laughs.*]

BF: Are you saying that this focus on the mother-daughter relationship as it often happens is the result of the nuclear family?

GP: Yes, I think part of it is that. Also, for many women, compassion for the oppressed mother; for others, anger because that oppression was handed on. The mother also enforced foot-binding, clitoridectomies, and obedience to husband. The nuclear family does have something to do with it. All of those intense focuses are like that. So I think this was sort of broadened out for me. Somehow or other if I felt mad at my mother, I went to my grandmother; if I felt mad at my aunt, I went to my mother.

BF: And you also had more than one role model in a way?

GP: Yes. My sister to this day is a very powerful person in my life—she's eighty-three now—so much so that people laugh at me. They say that when I talk to my sister I use an entirely different voice [*laughs*], especially my husband laughs. So there is that kind of thing. But there is also the fact that I haven't dealt with a great deal of that. It's no question about it.

BF: Do you like to be identified as an ethnic writer? A woman writer, a regional writer? Any of these categories?

GP: I don't care. I'm perfectly happy to be called a woman writer. I've done this argument in another panel in California two weeks ago with a young woman who said she did not want to be a woman writer. She would be marginalized, trivialized, and so forth. My only answer was "They'll marginalize you and trivialize you no matter what you call yourself." It's not because you say you're a woman writer. It's because they say, "What is this? A woman wrote it?"

BF: You said somewhere the difference between male and female writing is in content, not in style.

GP: Well, some of it is in style. I mean some writing seems to be, you know, like harder, and some seems softer. I know a lot of people feel that there's a great difference, but I can't. I don't know. Maybe in other languages it's true.

BF: But just think, for instance, about your own work and Christa Wolf's *Cassandra*. I don't know anything comparable in male literature.

GP: That's true. But I think a lot of it is subject. Joyce was a great model to me because I think of him as a much more female writer. I think if you move away from Stephen Dedalus to Leopold Bloom, you see that, you feel that in him. What he was to his wife is another story, but we can't talk about that. [*Laughter.*] I mean he liked her, and that's good enough I suppose. It's a start.

But I do think that a lot of it is subject matter. Somebody could sit down and prove to me that I was wrong. I'm wide open on that. I'm not opinionated. But I'm not able to totally see it. I see it in relationships. I see it at meetings. I see it in all of that, and so it should probably be reflected in the work. But I can't swear to it, that's all.

BF: But don't you have the feeling that there is maybe an international community of women writers who are concerned about the same kinds of things and have tried to develop a form to suit these concerns?

GP: Listen, I not only think there's an international community of women writers, I'm working on it. You really should know about what we are trying to develop right now: from PEN, the PEN organization, where we had our own personal struggle in our own country to create a women's committee, for lots of reasons, including the fact that most of the panels, discussions, and so forth would be almost entirely men. Something even worse than last night. There would be only one woman among a dozen men. So there's that. And then my friend Meredith Tax, who's extremely energetic and bossy and driving, after she got on the board of PEN, got to go to international meetings, which I just didn't want to go to anymore. But anyway she extracted from international PEN, which is run by mostly an old-guy-bloc from France, an international women's committee. I see those things very practically, very pragmatically.

SO: Are you a Jewish writer?

GP: Yes.

SO: Do you consider your writing Jewish-American literature?

GP: Not exactly. But the particular sound of the language as I and others like me speak it, and the disharmony of our experiences, and the strong baseline on which we depend—from before Chaucer, including the King James Version of the Bible, Whitman, Dickinson, Rukeyser, Auden, Thoreau, Cather, Joyce (not to mention the Russians in translation, et cetera)—make American literature, to which the strong Hispanic rhythms are being added.

SO: Do you, then, see yourself primarily as an American writer or rather as part of an international writers' community?

GP: Well, I think as a child of immigrants in a sense, of European immigrants. I am by birth, language, literary tradition an American writer. As a very strong feminist, which I wasn't when I began writing my first book but became, I know there is an international women's community, and I hope to be a part of that. And I think we have obligations to develop, maybe just translate and publish, those voices in other countries. I mean to help free those female voices. Just as you said, I mean, tell stories. Oh, by the way, another example of women's writing would be Elsa Morante in the book *History*. That's another great book that really no man could write.

BF: I agree. Your stories often celebrate communities of women and children. There's hardly ever hate, jealousy, spite, isolation between women and among women which makes communities of women unbearable for many women. Is that just not your experience, or are you aware of that?

GP: No. I'm aware of two things. First of all, they do get mad at each other. I mean I have this story "Friends," in which an old friendship ends, and other stories where friendships end for all kinds of reasons. I don't think hatred sets in, but the friendships do end. But I remember talking to Russian women and all they could tell me about was that women would never get together, they would scratch each other's eyes out. But I think that's not true. I think there's no more anger or competition among women than there is among men. Now that may just be where I live and in my life. But the men seem in some ways a hell of a lot more competitive with each other. They kill each other—economically or actually. They do it a different way; women would be more personal.

BF: I agree. But in my village the women usually gossip about each other. There's not much help they give each other. And their loyalty is to their husbands in the first place. And in your stories the women get together and they help each other and . . .

GP: Well, first of all, one of the stories really began by my writing about women without husbands. I think that has something to do with it. I mean you hit on something that I didn't think of quite that way. I worked with an awful lot of gay women, too, you know, who also aren't that nice to each other. Most of those women, especially in the early stories, are pretty much alone. Or they are mad at men, and they are bound by common bad experiences with men. They have been insulted in one way or another.

SO: Where do you situate yourself in the contemporary literary scene?

GP: It would be up to critics to say that. You know there are a lot of writers who think about that and speak about that. I don't even know what the contemporary literary scene is, exactly.

SO: Are you writing for a specific audience?

GP: I don't consciously do that. No, I don't. Well, I think that so much of writing comes from a primary longing to tell, not a story but to tell. I want to tell you this, you know? In my book of poems I think I have a poem about how it begins as a child. You come home and say, "Listen Ma, I want to tell you this," you know. And that's a primary thing—'I want to tell you this." I know it is first the mother and then whoever else is home. Then it's your best friend—"I want to tell you this." And then as time goes on, you don't think who you want to tell, but you do think this is the way it is and I have to put it down. So your who-you-want-to-tell is broadening. But it doesn't mean that you are going to change your work for that unknown out there.

BF: Do you know who your readers are?

GP: I think that any woman who doesn't know that she is supported by the women's movement in any country is fooling herself. Because it doesn't matter whether she is a feminist or not. People will read her and be angry at her, or they will read her and be glad. But women will read her, I know they will. But I know men read me a lot too because I get, in a funny way, more letters from men than women.

BF: Do you read reviews of your work?

GP: Reviews? Sometimes.

BF: Are you influenced by them in any way? I mean do you get annoyed at them?

GP: Sometimes I get annoyed, yes. I remember my second book, which really wasn't even all that political. But they said everything was too political. I wrote a letter back to the *Times,* just simply making a point that in any other country in the world you would be laughed at if you weren't political. And all this stuff was coming up from South America at the time, you know. Yet they would tell me: not here, not in this country; there is no such thing as political writing in the U.S. There should not be. Whereas you are reading madly stuff from Middle Europe and South America.

BF: Marge Piercy said at one point that the reviews in the *New York Times* can make a book or break it in a way. Do you agree?

GP: Absolutely. It's worse for the theater because so much money is put into the theater, and a play costs hundreds of thousands of dollars, and many people's careers can just be ended by one son of a bitch. The *Times* is very influential, but other things are too.

SO: Is it difficult to support yourself by writing?

GP: Oh, I can't.

SO: If you are not dependent on writing as a means of support, of course, it's easier. You are under less pressure to produce. It does make a difference for your art, doesn't it?

GP: Well, it means that I write when I really have to, pretty much. But once you start writing, you keep writing. You don't end it. It is true that if I have a deadline—like I had to finish some of those poems at a certain point—I did really not do a thing but stay in my room and work. But my husband is a writer, and he has a lot of trouble being published and is not depending on it at the same time for a living, but he still works like hell. So what I mean is, when you're a writer, you're a writer.

SO: But still, I think of women writers in the nineteenth century, when it was even worse than it is today . . .

GP: They wrote because it was one of the few means for them to make a living, as when I was a typist and made no living at all. And then when my book came out, I began to teach. I made a modest living there. My books have been in print really since 1959, and I'm very fortunate. I won't say a bad word about whether I am making money or not [*laughs*] because I consider it that I am just so fortunate. I mean that's a large payment to me at this time of my life. So on this book [*Long Walks and Intimate Talks*] I won't make a penny. [Since this interview I did make some happy royalties.]

SO: Something that I noticed in your stories is that your female characters all seem to enjoy sexuality and don't seem to have any problems with their sex life. For many women this is still a very painful, if not the most painful area. Why do you portray sex as unproblematic?

GP: Well, partly I think that when I began writing about this I guess I was in my mid-thirties, and I found sex pretty unproblematic. That's plain and simple. [*Laughter.*] And so did most of my friends. A number of the women who became gay later on became so partly because they had been gay to begin with or because of particular sexual experiences. People get divorced and fall for some other guy or some other woman, I mean as far as I can see. I am just thinking of Andrea Dworkin. I have really known Andrea since she was very young. I have known her since she was about eighteen years old. I used to love her very much. She was very dear to me. I mean when she writes about sexual life, it's horrible. And she did have some horrible experiences, you know, but I am not writing about her. That's all I can say. For me I really want to celebrate sexuality.

SO: Because that's the way you feel about it?

GP: And because I want to celebrate it. Because I think it's one of the greatest things invented [*laughs*], and it may be a pure invention that it is so great. I could be wrong, and Andrea could be right. But I think it should be. One of the things that bothers me with a lot of my sisters in movements that I have worked with is that their anger with men really has turned them not against men, which is all right as far as I am concerned, but against sex in general, so that even their lesbian experiences don't strike me as so hot as far as that's concerned.

BF: I think that everybody would want to celebrate sexuality. I think that wasn't our point. It's just that it isn't that easy for most women. And I don't mean in the way Andrea Dworkin writes about it. I mean it's just not that easy to go to a bar, as in one of your stories, and pick up any man there, buy him a drink or two, and have a good time with him.

GP: As far as I can see, she doesn't do too much of that, going to bars. But whether it's good sex or not I didn't deal with. [*Laughter.*] I think I wasn't even talking so much about sex as relationships with guys that were extremely difficult. Well, I don't know. It's really what you read, not what I say.

BF: Let's talk about your new book, *Long Walks and Intimate Talks*. It strikes us as quite different from *Later the Same Day.*

GP: Oh, it is different. It's an altogether different thing. It's made up of things that were like articles that I wrote. Most of them were not written for this book.

BF: It's more overtly political than the rest of your work.

GP: Yes, very specifically so. This book was originally a calendar for the War Resisters' League.

SO: The entire book?

GP: No, not the entire book. There's more in this, but all the things about El Salvador; those long poems were written specifically for that calendar. And the little essays or whatever you want to call them, pieces—some of them were written for different journals like *Mother Jones* or *Seven Days* or something like that.

BF: If you put together another collection of stories, would your stories be less political than the ones in there?

GP: Well, I would probably use some of those in there. I would use "Midrash on Happiness" and I would use "Three Days and a Question." I consider those stories. But I think they are the only ones I consider really full stories. So I would use those two stories in a collection of stories.

SO: Are you working on a book of stories at the moment?

GP: Yes. I'm writing some stories. I have another half or dozen or so of which I probably like about three. And I have another collection of prose pieces also.

SO: Do you feel that your writing has changed over the years?

GP: Not when I write stories. I don't feel I have in those two little stories or in *Later the Same Day.* I don't know. Again, you know, I'm not the judge of that. It's like you're getting older, right? Until you look in the mirror you think you're you. [*Laughs.*] It turns out you're not you anymore. But then you go away from the mirror and you're you.

SO: Is your poetry more personal as compared to your fiction?

GP: Well, my poems are more personal, a lot. But at one time I wrote only extremely personal poems, and now I think some of the poems in there represent political feelings, but even so they are personal.

BF: You published a book of poetry in 1992, *New and Collected Poems*. For a while you didn't want to publish your poetry because you thought it was too literary in a sense.

GP: Well, it was.

BF: What has changed?

GP: Well, just as I learned how to write stories from poetry—I've used the expression before—I went to school to poetry to learn how to write, to learn how to move language around, give it some zip. [*Laughs.*] But from writing stories I learned also how to bring that other language into poetry—that language of family and street, that more human, daily language.

BF: What about a novel now?

GP: I don't know. It's probably too late. When I listen to these guys reading their novels [*laughter*], I get sort of, you know, I get interested. I just think, well, I'm going to write a novel. It would be different than those—proving what you said. [*Laughter.*]

BF: Do you keep a diary?

GP: Not really. I keep pieces of paper.

BF: Could you imagine yourself writing your autobiography?

GP: No, I really couldn't. No. I have a couple of books written about me where I talk a lot and they ask me a lot of questions. And then they have gone ahead and looked stuff up. I can't see me writing an autobiography. I mean it seems so stupid. [*Laugh-*

ter.] You have to feel like you are telling the world something. I feel I'm doing it when I write the way I write.

BF: Did you read Simone de Beauvoir's autobiography? Were you interested in that? I mean a lot of women read her; even if they haven't read any other women's literature, they read Simone de Beauvoir's.

GP: Yes, I read it, but again it was a whole other life. Part of my life or what I've been interested in is staying this close to the people, if I can put it that way, to ordinary life, to daily life in some way. So she really did not have that much to tell me except that I was interested in her. I was interested, but I saw here is this woman who really wanted the absolute opposite of ordinary life, whereas that's the opposite of me.

BF: Well, she is in a way the archetype of the female intellectual who lived it all—the big culture, the big politics.

GP: She lived all that under some guy's thumb. [*Laughs.*] Under a generous thumb. [*Both laugh.*]

SO: Could you describe your relationship to language?

GP: Well, I partly did by saying I really went to poetry to learn, to learn how to write. I like language. I have written a lot of poems about language here and there. I just think about language a lot.

SO: Do you feel that you shape language, or do you feel that you are shaped by language?

GP: Oh, I think both things happen. What I want to say is how interesting it is to be brought up with a couple of languages around you. There is something about getting these two tunes, three tunes, in your ear. And English is very receptive to this. I mean English really warmly receives all these other languages. At least it does in the United States at the present time. So I feel that my language was shaped by the fact that in my house normally Russian was spoken. English was spoken. You never knew when people were going into one language or another. And Yiddish less so because only my grandmother spoke that. So these languages kind of speak to one another. They address one another in the nicest ways, and I think that's one of the things that happened. One of the best books that I have read in a long time is by a woman named Irini Spanidou, and it is called *God's Snake*. She's Greek. I just mean that she had that Greek and English coming together, and it gave it a new tune somehow.

BF: Do you think there is a trace of Russian in your stories?

GP: I can't call it a trace of Russian. I would just say that it was in my ear. There are inflections that are either Yiddish or Russian or something like that that are probably there and that people recognize. Probably better than I recognize because I'm used to it being me talking.

BF: Did you ever consider language to be male? Like you couldn't work in it because it belonged to men?

GP: What? Language?

SO: Some feminist theorists have this idea that language is male.

GP: My mother and my sister talked to me a great deal. I know that theory. I think too much is taken away from us by those theories, by many of those theories. It's as though we are nothing; we are just putty in the hands of fate. Because women have struggled in different ways and do talk to their babies. I mean who the hell talks to those goddamn babies but mamas. Pap comes home once in a while and says a few . . . My father was a very busy man. He worked very hard, in a poor neighborhood. He was marvelous and all that, but he didn't . . . When I got up in the morning and ran into my grandmother's room, she talked to me. When I was a baby, it was my sister and my mother who talked to me. I don't see it really. I would say that men take female language (I'm just making this up right now; I've never said this before); I would say that it's very probable that little boys who are very tender—and I have a son and a daughter; little boys are the tenderest things in the world—that little boys as they grow older grow out of their female language and go into the male world, where adult men have re-created female language. I like that. That's a good theory. [*Laughter.*] That's as good as the other one, isn't it? Where men take that language really and turn it into a means to make war and do other bad things. [*Laughter.*]

SO: In your most recent collection, *Long Walks and Intimate*

Talks, you have a poem entitled "It Is the Responsibility." In this poem to be a woman seems like a moral, political objective. Actually, there is a line that reads "It is the responsibility of the male poet to be a woman." Could you elaborate on that?

GP: Well, what happened was when I was writing the poem, I wrote "It is the responsibility of the male poet to be a woman." I think I wrote that line first. And I sort of knew that everybody would think that the next line would be "It is the responsibility of the female poet to be a man." So I just couldn't do it because I didn't think it was true. [*Laughter.*] So I guess I just wrote it because I thought it was true. I thought that, for all the reasons we have talked about so far, a man poet ought to be able to be a female poet; I mean he's got to think like a woman. And really it would do him a lot of good. On the other hand there's no reason for women to change. Oh, people get very mad at me for that. That poem has created more anger at me than almost anything else I have ever written.

SO: Really?

GP: Oh yes. It's so funny.

SO: Do you perceive women as more peaceful than men?

GP: I think by history, by culture, not by birth, you know. We have a one-year-old grandgirl who is quite nutty and wild and bopping people on the head and everything. No, I wouldn't say that I think that women are more peaceful, but I will say that I think that men are quite crazy at this present time. And I don't mean my own man or my son or lots of people that I know, but I mean the amount of blood, rage in the world, which is not women doing it at all. I mean more women are being killed. Women and children. You read the papers—more women and children have been killed in Yugoslavia and all through there. And dying in Somalia. It's a male madness that's been let loose in this world right now, as far as I can see. And where it comes from I don't know. I don't think women are more peaceful; I just think men are more warlike. It seems that way if you just listen to the radio. It's not a theory. It's what we actually see and read.

One of the things that always bothers me is when women in political movements that I've been involved in, like Central America and Palestine or something like that, when the women say, "I wish I had another two sons to give. I'm the mother of heroes." That infuriates me when women do that, and I think that I always want to say to them, "You go be a hero and a martyr if you're so hot for it, but don't be giving away your boys' lives." But I notice that they aren't going around being heroes and martyrs. They say, "Son, you go be a hero." So it's a hard question to answer because deeply I don't want to believe that men are more warlike. But I think that just pragmatically, from reading the paper every day, I'd say so far.

BF: But whenever a war is going on, there are women supporting the war effort at home.

GP: Of course there are, and one hates that. And yet for the First World War women from all countries tried to get together to stop it. There were women in Yugoslavia. I had lists of their names—of women and also a list of writers and intellectuals who just all begged them to stop. There were plenty of men who begged them to stop, that's true, who were horrified by it all. But something goes wild. I used to make jokes of it. I used to say well, that's because they don't know what to do in the afternoon after work. I don't think, for instance—you know we have this thing about being drafted into the army and stuff like that—I don't think women should be drafted into the army. I think men should not. So my feeling is that in certain areas they should be equal with us, not we with them.

SO: What does feminism mean to you?

GP: It means a couple of things. First it means you begin to understand you have a lot in common with other women. It's like a class thing. This class of women is a group of people that you have a good deal of life in common with. And it begins at that point. And then you begin to think about how the world is organized and what your position in it is, socially, and you understand what a patriarchal society you are living in, and it's not yours basically.

BF: Were you active in a women's liberation group from the beginning?

GP: Well, somewhat. You see I was in the peace movement. Probably because of the Vietnam War. And unlike many young women I was already working with a lot of women in it and also with several very unusual men, older mostly. A lot of the young women in the peace movement were really just pushed around by SDS (the student organization). That is, Meredith Tax or Marge Piercy were pushed around by these guys, these young fellows in these student movements, who were really not shallow because they were very smart, but callow and full of male beans and ambition and so forth. And accustomed to or forced to play a certain role. I think the women's movement has done a lot for men, a tremendous lot for them. For men who paid attention it has taken some of the burden of machoism off their backs, which is a terrible burden to bear. If you think about it, it's horrible. It's horrible to have to be that kind of person in order to be a person.

BF: A lot of men don't seem to recognize that because there is this backlash now. Marilyn French was here with her book *The War against Women*. It's like a lot of men say, "Women are responsible for everything that's wrong in my life."

GP: Yes, but they were saying that before. I talked to her about it. I like her very much.

SO: What about that backlash? I mean Robert Bly's book and people like that. Is it just something that is puffed up by the press?

GP: A lot of it is puffed up, but a lot of it is true. You can't expect men not to respond to a lot of criticism. All of those guys from the West talk about Toni Morrison. I can't tell you how it affects me. I am so upset with them. Jesus Christ, you know. Anyway, the men are a class that privileges have been taken away from, and they don't understand that. They think it's ordinary life that's been stolen, and it's like they have lived in this room and you have said, "We'd like to have one third of the room," and they go out of their minds naturally because they have been lying all over the place. [*Laughter.*]

SO: It's been like this all the time.

GP: Yes, it's natural, but we fight back. When she says there is a backlash, that doesn't mean that the women aren't there to fight that backlash. The press doesn't say it so much, but there was a meeting with Anita Hill in New York, and they had room for about eight hundred people. And there were thousands of women who just came to that one half-day conference to hear her. And then I've been going to meetings with a group called Action Committee. They meet every single Tuesday. This is just an ordinary meeting of an organization, and between two hundred and four hundred people meet every single Tuesday. [These meetings and actions have continued since we spoke.] So there's a backlash to the backlash if I can put it that way. It encourages me very much. That's true where I live in New England as well, where the women's movement was kind of pleased with itself and dormant for a while and has suddenly got mad, and women have begun to get together again.

BF: You have got a little piece in here. One of your conversation pieces where the narrator talks to her mother-in-law on her deathbed about women's lib. She comes down the next morning and says, "Those young women—what wonderful lives they're going to have." Would you agree?

GP: Yes, I do. I think it's much better for you guys than it was for me. I mean it was much better for my daughter except for AIDS, which wrecks everything. That business of AIDS does terrible things. It prevents people from naturally loving one another, and it makes people who have ceased to love one another stick together. Both terrible things.

SO: Are your children feminists?

GP: My daughter is. My son is a little backlashed [*laughter*] but not much. Not too much.

SO: Apart from being a feminist you characterize yourself in this book as a cooperative anarchist. I like the term very much. And a combative pacifist. Which of these things is most likely to get you into trouble?

GP: As a combative pacifist I have gotten into more trouble than as a cooperative anarchist.

SO: What are the current projects politically that you are involved in?

GP: I have been very involved in a lot of Jewish stuff too, and that's very interesting because again it is mostly women. It is the women in Israel called Women in Black, who have been fighting, who have been vigiling week after week after week. And we have our own Women in Black in New York and even in Vermont and in California; only we don't wear black, that's the only thing. But we really vigil for that. Now that's part of bringing together the peace movement and the women's movement because it's mostly women who are doing it. One of the really interesting things is that, for instance, in contacts with Palestinian women we have heard them say now that they won't allow to happen to them what happened to the Algerian women—after the revolution everything was turned back. Who knows? But those are the international contacts where people help each other out to understand things. I have been involved in that as a writer and as a woman and things like that pretty much. I have moved up to the country, so my life is a little peculiar.

BF: What is your relation to Israel?

GP: I'm not a Zionist and I never was. But I don't want them destroyed. I really don't. I do think there should be two states there. I think they should behave decently. They shouldn't act like such pigs. I'm very happy about the elections, though God knows what they'll finally mean.

BF: I was surprised.

GP: I was surprised. I think they were surprised too. I think people are tired of those rotten settlements. Those people are awful. And do you want to know something? They're mostly Americans. If not mostly at least in a large percentage.

BF: How did you feel about coming to Germany?

GP: I've come a number of times and probably the first time was strange. I wanted to look into every face and see some truth. What happened was that Germans often began the conversation, and in the end I wondered how I would bear such a burden. At the same time I come from a racist country full of denial of its history and live among Christians who suffer some mild form of antisemitism at least and a more virulent form of race hatred. I am interested in history and how the generations make it, then tell it. I was glad to see hundreds of Germans come out in protest of the foreign bashing. If five thousand had come into the streets after Kristallnacht, the world's history since would have been different.

SO: Let us return to women's experiences. You said somewhere that women who don't have children are missing out on a fantastic experience.

GP: I didn't say it like that.

SO: You said, "I think it's a shame that it has become almost a fashion not to have children." Do you still think it's necessary to have a child of one's own?

GP: Oh no, no. I never thought that. My sister has no children. But I do think relation to children is important. And I don't think people have to have children. My daughter has no children. I wanted to. It was easy for me because there was no political opposition to it. [*Laughter.*]

SO: On the contrary!

GP: On the contrary, right! So I didn't put it off. I do think a relation to children is a wonderful thing. I think a relation to old people . . . I think that you can't live a single-generation life. I mean you can, but, one, you don't learn enough from it, and two, it's more boring. You can get into fights with the generation that's ahead of you, and your children you certainly get into fights with. So you get into struggles with them. They are illuminating always. And you see what's ahead of you and you see what's in back of you. I think you have a sense of time. To me children are extremely interesting, but that's me personally, and it's not what I think other people must feel.

SO: It should be an option for women to decide that they don't want to have children.

GP: Well, I would fight to the death for their right not to have children. I mean as far as the whole abortion thing is concerned, that's one of my major concerns.

SO: So you have been active on abortion?

GP: Oh yes, I have. That's a very big struggle in the United States. God knows what's going to happen. I mean we're really dealing with maniacs. There is this other little piece in there [*Long Walks*] about what it was like for us when there was no abortion allowed. It was just simply sheer oppression.

BF: Do you think that Pro-Lifers have a chance in the States?

GP: They're very strong, but they've been beaten back in every town. I mean women have really been there and not allowed them. But they are part of the whole fundamentalist movement that is crawling across the whole world, and we have to stop them.

SO: You're right. It's the same in Germany too.

GP: Oh, I bet.

SO: In your writing children always are a sort of promise, the hope for the future, new beginnings.

GP: I don't think you begin again. Sometimes when you are with children, you feel old. You feel worse than anything.

BF: Well, we wanted to ask you how you feel about turning seventy this year? What does old age mean to you?

GP: Well, if you have the book, it has a couple of hard poems in there. Golda Meir was asked that question: "We hear you don't mind getting older?" And she said, "That's true, but I never said it was a pleasure." I can't think of a better answer in this sense. I mean you get older and your time gets shorter on this earth; and if you happen to like this earth, you really get a little gloomy about having to leave it. There are a lot of things one is curious about—like what will come next in the world's life—and very angry that you won't know. And you feel that if you turn your back by dying, it'll get very bad behind your back, or something like that. The whole world will blow up, and you'll never know that's what happened. You couldn't stop it. If you'd only been there, you would have stopped it. No, I think if you're healthy . . . I'm pretty healthy. My husband is pretty healthy. We really like each other a lot, and our kids are in fairly good shape. But if you get old in another way, it's very bad. If you don't have money, it's terrible. Not that we have a lot, but I don't have to worry really, and I'm still working.

BF: So you don't worry too much?

GP: You do; you can't help it. You know, not really worry. You wake up early afraid sometimes, but you do sometimes when you're thirty-three and a half [*laughs*], and you don't know what's coming, right?

FIVE

ISHMAEL REED

interviewed by Wolfgang Binder and Harald Zapf

Ishmael Reed is one of the leading African-American writers in the United States. He was born in 1938 in Chattanooga, Tennessee, grew up in Buffalo, New York, and attended the University of Buffalo. Mr. Reed has taught at several universities, among them Harvard and Yale, and has been a professor since 1967 at the University of California, Berkeley. He lives today in Oakland, California.

Since the mid-sixties, he has been writing novels, poems, and essays. His experimental novels are distinguished by an imagination that appears both surreal and satirical. Mr. Reed, who describes one important aspect of his writing as "Neo-HooDooism," is especially interested in the myths, magic, and rituals that live outside the Western culture. His third novel, Mumbo Jumbo *(1972), helped to continue the innovative African-American aesthetic tradition of the Harlem Renaissance. With his independent African-American aesthetic, which he poses as an alternative, he criticizes the repressive Western tradition with biting irony.*

WB/HZ: Ishmael Reed, you grew up in Buffalo, New York. What is characteristic of this city in terms of ethnicity, politics, and culture?

IR: At that time the population was culturally and ethnically mixed. Although African-Americans lived there too, it was mostly a mix of European culture. The Poles were the largest ethnic group in Buffalo. There were probably more Poles there than in Warsaw. Finally, they realized their political power and ran the city and are still running it. There was also a large German ethnic population. In addition to that, there is a very strong Irish-Catholic and Italian-American influence to this day. After I had left Buffalo in 1962 for New York City, writers like Robert Creeley and the Beats came into Buffalo. In the meantime, there are hip areas in the city. Before that, Buffalo was merely an automobile manufacturing city, one of these typical steel towns.

During the Civil War, Buffalo was a center of abolitionist activity because it was the last stop before Canada, which I allude to in my novel *Flight to Canada*. All the celebrities of the abolitionist movement, like Frederick Douglass, came to Buffalo. William Wells Brown, the first African-American novelist, also lived there.

WB/HZ: You already began to write as a young person. Do you remember some individuals who encouraged you to write or who influenced the style of your writing?

IR: I began to write for a small community newspaper at the age of thirteen. The editor had black journalists on the staff who were very articulate and intellectual. From them I learned a lot about civil rights and the freedom struggle of the African-Americans. Then, at the university, I was encouraged to write by a man named Scott. He was very impressed by a short story I wrote, which was passed around the faculty. They were going to offer me a scholarship, but my stepfather wouldn't sign the papers. He came from the old southern tradition where people are very reticent about signing documents. I left the university after two and a half years and went back to the newspaper where I worked as a kid. At that time, Malcolm X came through. I interviewed him on radio. His way of talking changed my style. My writing became more direct. I was also very impressed by experimental writers like Nathanael West. He wrote in an unconventional manner that I had never seen before. I said, if I'm ever going to write, I will write in that style. I was also very influenced by a man named Vester. He was a German, a German band leader, a band teacher. I spent most of my time in the band room.

WB/HZ: What kind of music did you play?

IR: Well, we played all kinds of things: we played Stan Getz arrangements. I played the trombone. One of the people who performed there was "Red" Don Menza. He is a very well known jazz musician. He is now playing with Maynard Ferguson. We played in New York together.

WB/HZ: So you have a musical background, too?

IR: Certainly. I played the violin in high school. I played in a string quartet—Schubert, Mozart, all this. I enjoyed it very much. So when they say, well, this man is out of the Western civilization, I probably know more about classical Western music than, say, the people who are leading the antimulticultural fight.

WB/HZ: You have just mentioned Malcolm X. Do you have any idea who killed him?

IR: I heard rumors, nothing solid. I merely heard that the government had tried to promote conflict between Elijah Muhammad and Malcolm X, the same thing they did to the Black Panthers.

WB/HZ: In his essay "Down at the Cross," James Baldwin had a critical but fair look at the Black Muslims and especially at Elijah Muhammad. What do you think of him?

IR: I have a lot of respect for Elijah Muhammad. In the research for my new book, *Japanese by Spring,* I found out that he was against World War II. At that time there were pro-

Japanese groups in America, and Elijah Muhammad was one of them. Finally, he went to jail for five years for his seditious activity.

WB/HZ: You left New York in 1967 in order to go to the West Coast. Do you think that this was advantageous to your life and your work?

IR: I left Buffalo because I was looked upon as a kind of eccentric fool. Then, in New York, I was getting too much affection. That can be very crippling. I needed more anonymity, which I finally found on the West Coast. In terms of art and culture, Manhattan was wonderful, though. Everything concerning multiculturalism began there. My friends and I were talking about things like "international mind-minding." After I had moved to Berkeley, Víctor Hernández Cruz, with whom I founded the Before Columbus Foundation in 1976, also came to the West Coast.

WB/HZ: You have been teaching at the University of California in Berkeley since 1968. What are you teaching there at the moment?

IR: I'm teaching something called "Introductory Verse," but I hide everything in there. In my opinion the students often have been miseducated. For example, they often deny that Picasso's work is close to African art. Europeans depict a Moor as very dark-skinned. To academics in the United States the Moors are white. They don't want to entertain the possibility that African-American people had anything to do with culture. For me, it is very important to invalidate myths like that in a course.

WB/HZ: Let us get back to the publishing house, the Before Columbus Foundation. Did you plan from the beginning to publish mostly authors from different ethnic groups, or did that develop?

IR: That developed. At first I published an anthology of black writers. In 1969 a book called *Necromancers from Now* was published. Frank Chin and Víctor Cruz were included there. *Necromancers* led to something called *Yardbird Reader* and *Quilt Magazine*. I also did an anthology of Californian poetry called *Calafia*. It was the first time that all these different cultures were together in one volume. You had to read about one hundred and twenty-five pages of introduction before you got to the first poem. There was an introduction for each ethnic group in order to show how rich the poetry is. *Calafia* is a forerunner of the kind of stuff I am doing now. Now I have my magazine *Konch,* which I operate out of my house. There are interviews in it in which people say things they would not be allowed to say in any other magazine publication.

WB/HZ: In your novel *Reckless Eyeballing* you attack the feminists and compare them to the right wing in politics.

IR: I always bring up the Nazi parallel because that scares them. I try to tell them, "Well, that's what you are practicing." Let's take the Willie Horton campaign as an example. He got out of jail and raped a woman. George Bush used that old image of the black man as a rapist in the election and won. The feminists went beyond that. They had pamphlets out saying: "If you like Dukakis, Willie Horton, or somebody like him, will be going from door to door all over America after your women." That was like a Hitler-type campaign.

WB/HZ: How do you assess the reporting of the Los Angeles uprisings? Did you comment on the incidents in the mass media yourself?

IR: I can't comment on that in the media in the United States. They want to talk to Michael Jordan. In the newspaper there are so-called free pages open to expression, but people like me can't get in there. In America, you can't really say what is on your mind, and when you do say it nevertheless, as I and some of my rebellious friends say it, they dismiss us as people who are mad.

The Nazis in America are pushing this thing called race and crime. There is a terrible tabloid called *New York Magazine,* which reminds me of the *Stürmer.* The editor, Joe Klein, says that the riots happened because of lack of morality and value in the black community. Analysts like Klein are just not looking at the average person in this community, which is poor, very conservative, very church-oriented, and very much for law and order. Most of them are working-class people. Chinese Americans are responsible for all the heroin going to black neighborhoods. Seventy percent of heroin in New York—"China white," this lethal stuff—is pushed by the Chinese Americans, and the police say, "Well, that's such a secret society . . . we can't get the evidence."

WB/HZ: Was it made clear in the media that it wasn't only an uprising of African-Americans?

IR: I think the line in the commercial media was that it was blacks. African-Americans are looked upon as a burden to society, just like the Jews in Nazi Germany. As a matter of fact, the riot was a Latino riot. Fifty-two percent of the people who were arrested were Latinos. Two thousand Latino businesses were destroyed. Jesse Jackson even hinted at the fact that a lot of these businesses were burned by the owners in order to collect insurance. In Berkeley and San Francisco, we had a white riot. The chief of the police said that he wished that the white rioters would behave as well as the African-American community. The white conservative news producers, though, projected it as a black riot. The media in the United States has to be diversified now. Up to now, the media has been dominated ninety-five percent by people with the same background and the same forefathers. Only five percent are from other ethnic groups, like blacks and Latinos.

WB/HZ: How do you rate the power and the influence of the media in America?

IR: I said in Berlin the other day that Ted Turner is probably more powerful than Goebbels ever was. They have an enormous power. They malign certain unpopular groups and send these images all over the world. Some black columnist, who writes for the local *Herald Tribune,* went to Tokyo, turned on the TV, and there were black people on drugs on CNN. Everybody's finger-pointing at the black community. Blacks are treated as an enemy nation within the United States. We're the evil empire now.

WB/HZ: Could you comment on Protestantism in the United States?

IR: It is not the sort of Protestantism that you had in England. I did some investigations on the Puritan reformations. There is much material you can't get your hands on, and I understand now that what separated them from the Protestants in England was a big try to impose their stuff on everybody. The Puritans try to impose their ideas and beliefs on everybody. That's why the English put them out of the country. That's the Protestant legacy we are dealing with in the United States, and right now you're undergoing the Puritan interregnum that you had in England, where they banished theater, banished dancing, all that stuff. That is the Protestant legacy.

WB/HZ: In many of your books you stress syncretism a lot, both cultural and religious. Could you explain the importance of Haiti for your work?

IR: In Haiti, there are all those different African tribes together on one island, and that is where all their mythologies are fused. *Vodoun* is merely shorthand for what happens when you get all these people from different nations, pooling all their mythologies and languages. The developments in Haiti are examples of the kind of aesthetics that we achieved when we considered the multicultural study. I call it "Neo-HooDoo aesthetic." That's the reason why Haiti was important to us. Through our collaboration with different ethnic groups, we were introduced to things of our own culture that we hadn't been aware of before. I have seen parallels in their experience to ours, and we've illuminated their backgrounds as well. That is one of the positive things in multiculturalism.

WB/HZ: Very often, you use New Orleans as a metaphor and as a spiritual geography. Would you agree to the idea that New Orleans is a Caribbean town?

IR: I think so. The architecture, the cuisine, the style, it seems out of place in the United States. One reason why Hoodoo blossoms there is that the slaves were brought in from Haiti. The Mardi Gras is probably a Caribbean thing, too. The way the people dress there is typical of the Caribbean. North American Indians don't have that kind of stuff. I went to see the carnival in New Orleans. It is a mixture of French, Spanish, and African culture.

WB/HZ: Up to now, two CDs with your texts and the music of David Murray, Lester Bowie, Allen Toussaint, and other composers have been published. How did these projects come about?

IR: I didn't influence the music. Kip Hanrahan arranged and produced everything. He was the one who took my work and sent it to different composers. They read *Mumbo Jumbo* and were willing to set my stuff to music. I didn't hear the music until it was performed. The CDs were very popular in the college radio stations. For some time, Harvard station played it every day.

WB/HZ: What do you think of hip-hop?

IR: I like a lot of it. But some of the stuff is trash. Some rappers are really fascist. It is ironic that their antisemitic records are produced by Jewish producers. Before anything else, hip-hop is just capitalism. Rappers like Sister Souljah toy with a kind of pseudo-radicalism in order to sell a lot of records. They are all capital. Many hip-hoppers wear Marcus Garvey's colors and want separatism and sovereignty. They have more money available than Marcus Garvey ever had to carry out those plans. Why then isn't there a serious move toward African-American sovereignty? In my opinion, they are only playing with the idea of black nationalism. I like Michael Franti and the Disposable Heroes of HipHoprisy. I think they are going into a different direction.

WB/HZ: Similar to the Blaxploitation movies of the seventies, there is now a new wave of "black movies" in our cinemas. Have you seen some of them?

IR: Yes, I have seen *Boyz N the Hood,* and I don't think very much of it. In my opinion, the dialogue between the father and the son was mediocre. I think there was probably more time spent structuring the scenes of violence than the others. In the trailers, only the violent scencs were used. Singleton, the director, said that those scenes were used to get the audience to come and see that the movie was not about violence. I think *Deep Cover* is much better than *Boyz N the Hood.* That's an excellent movie. It took the crack trade all the way up to the White House. George Bush is also mentioned in this context. All in all I think that you have to give young black film makers like Spike Lee a lot of credit for beating that system because I think that film is very difficult to get into. Today, film has more power to influence than writing.

WB/HZ: How important is satire for you?

IR: I can go from issue to issue, from event to event in the United States, and I can have an ironic twist on it. The United States provides endless material for me.

SIX

LUCI TAPAHONSO

interviewed by Helmbrecht Breinig and Klaus Lösch

Luci Tapahonso, born in 1953, is a member of the Navajo tribe and grew up on the Navajo reservation in New Mexico. She has published several volumes of poetry, among them Seasonal Woman *(1981) and* A Breeze Swept Through *(1987). Her latest book,* Sánnii Dahataał: The Women Are Singing *(1993), contains both poetry and stories. Luci Tapahonso is an exception among contemporary American Indian authors because she reads and writes her tribal language. She uses both English and Navajo in her publications as well as in her readings. Besides numerous readings in the United States and Canada, the author has also presented her works on radio and television. Moreover, she is the author of a script for a film entirely in Navajo that presents the present-day life of the Navajo. Ms. Tapahonso is presently an assistant professor at the University of Kansas, Lawrence.*

HB: I'd like to begin with a question concerning "She Sits on the Bridge" in that anthology by Simon Ortiz. According to the subtitle, that anthology contains "short fiction," but your text is written in verse lines. Is it short fiction nevertheless? And would you call that your way of merging the oral tradition and modern fiction?

LT: No, I think that when Simon was looking for material for that, I didn't really have anything that was short fiction, and I told him I really didn't have any fiction that I wanted him to use. And he said, "Well, just give me anything that seems to be telling a story." And that was what I gave him. So I don't consider it fiction, actually. I think it is probably more prose than it is fiction. And I generally don't write short stories. Although where the story came from, the way the story began, would make a really wonderful work of fiction by itself. It's in very abbreviated form. If I *told* you the story, it would just be so different. It's a very scary story.

HB: So it's a condensed, a poeticized version. But it's a wonderful story, nonetheless. I mean, when you read it, you read it as a story although it's a poem; so somehow these two things go together, here.

LT: [*Murmurs affirmatively.*]

KL: I think there is an obvious storytelling quality in some of your poems, in "It Was a Special Treat," for example. It seems to me that it is more or less a story but in lines. Do you think that this proximity between poetry and storytelling is part of your tribal attitude?

LT: I think that it probably is. Because we were not really raised with people saying "You shouldn't do that," that sort of thing. But rather they would tell you stories. For instance, when my daughter and I were both coming to Europe, we had a ceremony. The medicine man told a lot of stories to my daughter; he told her a lot of stories about the creation, different parts of creation stories. And it was part of the ceremony but it was also for her to understand that she's coming over here as a Navajo person.

Generally, there is always a sense of closure but not necessarily in ending. It doesn't mean it's the end; it just closes that particular part of the story.

KL: A more general question, talking about your cultural background: How would you define yourself as a writer? Do you think of yourself as primarily a Native American writer? Or an American writer? Or a North American writer?

LT: I don't know. I guess, I don't really consider those labels. Sometimes people ask my daughters, "How does it feel to have a mother that's a writer?" And they say, "Well, we've never had another kind of mother." I think that certainly the perspective that I'm writing from is unique because there's not very many people who are writing from that kind of experience that I have. And in that way one can't avoid the label of being a Native American author. That is something that is unavoidable, no matter what you do because it is so distinct, and it is one that is not heard from very often. I think that the labeling, though, whether people say female writer, or poetess, or any way that they indicate gender, is unnecessary for the most part because I think that for Indian people writing it down doesn't really matter. I think that the kind of things that they are talking about and what they are writing about are the same. My work, the things I touch upon and the approach to it, is basically the same as Simon Ortiz's. Because, I think the culture that we come from matters. I would have to say, though, that this distinction is for writers that are raised in their own communities, that know their language, and that have a full understanding of where they come from. In those communities there, you don't have such distinctions of gender. You just aren't raised with those kinds of distinctions. So you could say that my work and Simon's work are very similar because of the themes and the approach that we take to things. Because of the culture that we were raised in it doesn't matter that he is a man and it doesn't matter that I am a woman. The same things are important to us. There are other Native writers, like for instance, Paula Gunn Allen, who really considers herself a feminist writer. Her approach is very different from mine because she's just been raised differently and is much more influenced by American society than I was at an early age.

HB: Talking about influence, you refer to Leslie Silko as a kind of teacher and mentor. Now she is, of course, the best-known example for the merging of the oral tradition and fiction by taking the mythic element right into the story, right to the level of action—for instance in *Ceremony,* which is clearly a narrative of contemporary events and at the same time some kind of mythic story. Do you try in your stories or in your narrative poetry—let's put it that way then—do you try to keep that more apart? Do you try to keep the mythic at a somewhat longer distance (as Simon also does) by putting it on the level of, say, reported experience, like in the story we mentioned before?

LT: I think it really depends on each piece individually. I think that "She Sits on the Bridge" is a story that's very common in many rural communities. It would be regardless of whether or not the community was a Navajo community or if it was one of the small Hispanic communities in northern New Mexico. They would have the same version of that same story because it is a classic road story. You know, this happens a lot in different places, so it's kind of a retelling of the story in that way. But the setting is Navajo, and that's what makes it different. When I am thinking of it as of something that could possibly be a poem, then the beginnings of it would be always in Navajo. My poems always begin first in Navajo. So whatever form, they begin in Navajo. This might be a certain phrase, like today, for some reason, I was thinking a lot about this phrase which would be "Jó 'akódaa jiníłei." It seems like I would think of something, and in the end I would just somehow put at the end of that: "Jó 'akódaa jiníłei." "That's what they would say," I guess that's the way you would translate this. And I began to realize that as that phrase came into my mind more and more, that somehow that was the beginning of a poem. That line was going to be significant. And when I put it down in English, "Jó 'akódaa jiníłei, Jó 'akódaa jiníłei, Jó 'akódaa jiníłei," the way that that would finally appear in English might be "That's what they would say," "*That's* what they would say," or it might be something else, like "A long time ago, they would say that a lot." So the English version would be different. However it finally ends up in English, the original part of it, the original thought, the spark of it, started in Navajo. And then that form somehow just carries over. Does that make sense?

KL: So you are writing poems in Navajo and in English. I suppose you feel more at home writing in Navajo?

LT: I think that there's a Navajo version of it, but then I have a hard time writing it in Navajo; Navajo is hard to write because I can't hear all the sounds of it. So then, when I'm writing it down, I become confused. I think, what's the correct way to write it? Sometimes I just leave it in Navajo. Sometimes I translate it into English, which is what I just did to that phrase. That would be the way it comes out in English. Even if I translate it directly, I think *that* English is different from standard English because of the fact that it is a translated line.

HB: How about your audience? I'm sure you have readers among the Navajo and, of course, in the general reading public. Do you react differently to your texts?

LT: Yes. Navajo people seem to like my work, it's really nice. People in New Mexico just have such an understanding of my work that other people don't. I think it has to do with land. I'm not sure. But Navajo people really appreciate my work. And a lot of times they would come and say, "You know that story you told about this and that . . ." (except they will never say "that poem"; they will always say "that story" even if it's a poem), "Well, you know, that story you told about this," and I would say "Yes," and they'd say, "Well, you know about five years ago, this is what happened to me." And they would tell me another story about that, and they would say, "Just remember that in case you're thinking of writing something else." They will come to me and help me with things. Yes, it's really neat.

HB: Of course, the problem with the audience is always their imagination, their capability of creating something in their minds. In your interview with Joe Bruchac you speak of poetry as a song, which, I quote, "creates a dance within a person's imagination." And that reminded me a lot of notions that Black Mountain poets also had, of the joining of the physical and the mental-spiritual. And in their case, it went in the direction of a kind of performance—you don't just read the text on the page but you have to perform it. Is that something you would also prefer to do, rather than just put it on the page?

LT: I don't know if it would be called performance. I think that it's in the *telling* of a story. If it is important to me, I would want to tell it in a way that would make it relate that. I wouldn't tell you in any manner, like just rushing through or like just saying it any way because, then, that would be disrespectful to you. But it would also be disrespectful of me in terms of how I'm using the language. It has to do not necessarily with performance, but it has to do with the perception of how a person values the words that we say. In Navajo, they say that when a baby is born, the first breath that they take is *The wind comes inside you,* and then you go [*inhales*]. And each of these fingertips, each of them has different color winds. And it starts here with black wind, blue, yellow, white, and pinto wind—that's kind of a mix, a mixed kind of colors. The little place on top of your head where your hair starts to grow, another wind comes in. These all enter into you when you're born, when you're a baby. And when the wind comes in at that time, then the dawn determines how long the wind's going to remain inside you, meaning how long you are going to be living here. So after that, each breath that a person takes—each time you breathe and each time you say something—it's just not yourself, but it's all those forces of the world. It's all the forces that create, too, that create thunder, tornadoes, light rain, real heavy rain; it has all those elements that come inside you. So each time you speak then, those things are there. And it's just not like—you know how people say "They're just talking," meaning "Don't pay attention to them"—it's not that view. So for me, when I'm telling a story—and this is not just me but this is the way that Navajo people are raised—when I tell a story or tell somebody about something, then it's important to think about each of the words that you use. So when you do that, then necessarily you give a lot of attention to the words that you choose, the phrasing that you use, what you emphasize, and then, if you do those things, it takes on its own rhythm, its own life. So it's not necessarily a performance.

HB: This is all very beautiful, but how do you manage to convey that in written form?

LT: I don't know if I convey it in written form. I think that in written form, each person reads it in their own way. So then you just have to let it go and hope that that happens. Some of the ways that I do it, too, are by using space and by using line breaks. Generally, I don't write in closed form. I use an open format. When I read, there's a song that goes with the poem, that doesn't appear on the page.

HB: I see some links with Black Mountain poetry, after all, because they also had a notion, as did Ginsberg, that your breath, your actual physical breathing as a poet, enters into your written text somehow and in this way will hopefully also reach the reader.

LT: [*Murmurs agreement.*]

KL: Do you think that this responsibility in using language is something cultural? That it is one of the differences between tribal culture or Navajo culture and white culture, as some of the other Native American writers expressed it?

LT: I think that it probably differs from place to place. One of the things that they have always said to me was "Remember that you're one of us" and "Remember that you're Navajo," which really means "You're not by yourself." So I think that sense of responsibility in my case is that maybe I'm the one that's writing them down, but they're not necessarily just mine; I didn't create all this stuff. As I said earlier, you know that I have a lot of help in different ways. So it's not an individual kind of thing. Nia Fransciso and Rex Jim are also Navajo writers, and we talked about this, and yes, that's the way that we feel. It has to do with even the way I introduced myself at the beginning [of my reading]. I sort of establish that I'm not by myself by saying that these are the people I was born for, this is the people that I am, these are my grandparents. These are all the ways I live in the world. So the responsibility of that enters into work, and that's why I don't use words that could be offensive because I don't think that's very important. Anybody can do that. That's probably why Ed Vega was disappointed [with my statement during our discussion]. [*Laughs.*] But that's not the way that I am.

HB: You also say that you link poetry and prayer. And you once said that there is no separation, and the way you are talking now, of course, also confirms that bringing together of things, that emphasis on totality. That reminds me somewhat of what Paula Gunn Allen wrote in "The Sacred Hoop." Do you think that she is right that in Indian thinking there are really no dichotomies, or is that an overharmonious view of things? Are there tensions nevertheless which you have to bridge?

LT: I think that there are tensions. I think that it is like what we talked about earlier in terms of what are advantages to having this, doing this, and what are disadvantages to it and that sort of thing. So I think that it is relative, too. I think that the approach that I'm aware of in terms of how you handle things that come up in life is made easier for me because of things that I was raised with and things that have always worked for people. But I'm also aware that there are other ways of doing things, too, that do not necessarily apply to that.

KL: What do you think about women's liberation?

LT: [*Laughs.*]

KL: Do you think that from your point of view you have already answered the question?

LT: Navajos are a matriarchal society. In Navajo they say your mother is your home. You never leave your mother; you always treat your mother really good because without your mother you would not even be here. When a Navajo man gets married, he moves in with his wife's family and leaves his own family. He then becomes responsible for his wife's family as well as his own mother. And I think, many times men are under much more pressure than the women are. It's a much more egalitarian society than American society is. And so all the concepts of women's liberation, I think, are things that were already dealt with in our creation stories.

HB: You are probably familiar with Jeanette Armstrong's attempts in British Columbia to establish a center for Native writers, the En'owkin School of Writing. Would you favor the establishment of similar centers and institutions in the United States? Would they be useful, particularly for the Navajo, or should there be, on the contrary, more emphasis on literature in the Navajo language?

LT: I'm not really familiar with the project in Canada. I don't know a lot of the details about it or what they are doing. I think that there are such places. You know, economically the country is right now in such a bad situation that this kind of project could not even be established. The projects that did even half of that or attempted to do that all operate on soft monies, and that kind of funding has sort of fallen out from under it. There are several places on the reservation that have curriculum centers and a place like a clearinghouse for all kinds of materials. There are Navajo-written textbooks, first-grade books that are in Navajo, all kinds of things. There is on the Navajo Reservation, Navajo Tribe, a Division of Cultural Studies that employs medicine men as some of the teachers that work in the schools. So I think on our reservation, there's the beginning of that. It certainly could be better, though I think, just realistically, it won't be until . . . depending on what happens with the next election as to how that can go. But now, under the Republicans, we have not done well.

HB: What does the commemoration date 1992 mean to you? Does it mean anything at all?

LT: I think that it allows us to realize that we have survived a lot. Ever since Europeans came to our continent, there have been various kinds of programs and various kinds of policies that were all designed to make sure that we would not exist anymore. Everything that has ever happened has been with that in mind. And I think that regardless of that it's amazing that we're all here.

At least for Navajos: that we speak our own language and that this system of religion is still in place. And that even that being the case, I can take part in American life as a full citizen. And I can have advantages of both sides. I think that at least in terms of commemorating that, I tend to look at it as a reaffirmation of the strength that people have, the resilience, and the fact that it's really an amazing thing that we are here, because of everything that has happened, most of which was not positive.

HB: One of the consequences of 1492 is multiculturalism. Would you say that everybody nowadays should aim at achieving something like a multi- or at least bicultural competency? Because obviously in your case, and in the case of others, this is such an advantage, such additional wealth.

LT: I think that it would be an advantage, but I think that for the most part the American mind-set is that English is good enough and that we don't need to know another language. That, besides, the whole world's going to be talking English pretty soon. And why would we want to do that? There seems to be an ethnocentric attitude. I don't think that that's possible. People won't buy that.

HB: I'm still interested in the question of communicating between one culture and another, especially in the case of a writer who's so strongly influenced by her cultural background—the place, the area, and the people—as you are. Do you try consciously to find ways of communicating things which are specific to your culture or your area, at least? For instance, the comparative importance of the mother's brother—as in that poem we talked about ["Hills Brothers Coffee"]—it is something we non-Navajos just would not know; that traditionally, culturally, this is a very important person in everybody's life there with the Navajo. Do you make an effort to give readers some help, or do you trust that they will pick up something?

LT: I think that most of the time it's not really a conscious thing. It's really what I think about the most, what is most meaningful to me; if suddenly for two or three days straight I really miss my uncle and I just keep thinking about him, then I will write about that, because to me that is the most important. And I think that if people will understand something about culture from that, then it's a good thing. But you know, I trust that the audience, a reading audience, can pick up on inferences that are made and that they are a fairly intelligent audience. Not very often do I sort of consciously write something that I think will tell something about the Navajos that I'd like people to know. Because most of the time I will see something, and I will think about what this would be in Navajo, or is there an equivalent of this in Navajo? Because that's just what would occur to me as a Navajo person. As I said, somebody might say, "Why don't you write something about this?" And they'd make me a suggestion, and maybe I will.

HB: I was thinking of that story "Snake Man," for instance. I was wondering if those negative associations connected with the snake there wouldn't be rather more appropriate for girls coming from a Christian background than from a Navajo background.

LT: We didn't even know enough about Christianity to know that was a negative thing. We didn't even know about Adam and Eve until way later than that. That was when I was in second or third grade. And that was the way I remember it. And maybe about three years ago I saw that girl Cathy, the one who used to walk to the cemetery, and we were talking about that. And I asked her, "Do you remember that?" She said, "I remember it vaguely, but," she said, "I thought it was a dream." And I said, "No, you used to walk over there."

HB: So it's just the group of you who made this up, it's not referring to a particular tradition of a "Snake Man" who would be evil or dangerous?

LT: That was just a name that we made for him because he was running around down there. I guess the shadow or something, that's what we thought. We just gave him that name.

KL: Talking about attending school, I wanted to ask you if you experienced the tension between what you learned within your family and what you were taught in school as strongly as other Native Americans did.

LT: If there was a conflict?

KL: This tension between what you were taught at home in your native culture and the Western civilization or teaching imposed upon you.

LT: I think that my experience was pretty typical for people of my generation. I think that we were sent to school unprepared because my parents didn't have that background to be able to prepare us for it. Their experiences had always been negative, too, but then they didn't have the preparation, they didn't know anything about Christian culture, religion, to tell us, "Now, those kinds of things are wrong" or "That's not so." But my mother learned fairly quickly when I would come home and I would start telling her about the devil and that Jesus could make thousands of fishes [*laughs*], you know, all this kind of funny talk. And she would say, "Those stories—go ahead and let them believe that. But that's not yours; you are a Navajo." [*Laughs.*] So she learned by what I learned.

HB: One last question: Can you see your books translated into German? Would you like that?

LT: I think that people here might have an appreciation of it just because of the way that the life-style is, where we were driving around today. And the appreciation people have for land and their concern for environment and surroundings. I think that my approach—in some fundamental way—is the same.

SEVEN

ED VEGA

interviewed by
Wolfgang Binder

Ed Vega is the pen name of Edgardo Vega Yunqué. Born in 1936 in Ponce, Puerto Rico, he moved at the age of twelve with his family to the Bronx in New York, where his father was a minister in the local Protestant community. Ed Vega is the author of numerous short stories, which have been published in two volumes, Mendoza's Dreams *(1987) and* Casualty Report *(1991), and of a novel,* The Comeback *(1985). He is considered the most literary among Puerto Rican writers writing in English. In many of his works, which are marked by whimsical humor and satirical wit, he has parodied such established literary traditions as the American success story and the ethnic autobiography.*

WB: Ed, when and where were you born?

EV: I was born in Ponce, Puerto Rico, on May 20, 1936.

WB: When did you leave the island?

EV: In March of 1949.

WB: Did your whole family move to the U.S.?

EV: When I was about ten years old, my father came to the United States—to this end I don't know why. He was a very adventurous man in a way, and he came, I think, to investigate the possibilities of our move to the United States. Then in 1948 I was sent to live with my uncle in Palmer, which is a very small town near El Yunque. My sister was sent to live with an aunt near the university. My father and mother left with our little brother, and a year later they sent for us.

WB: Where did they settle in the U.S.?

EV: My father was able to become the minister of a Hispanic congregation with different Protestant denominations, which had acquired after the war a beautiful German mini-cathedral.

WB: In which section of New York was that?

EV: In the Bronx, in the South Bronx, which was then predominantly an Irish neighborhood but had also German and Jewish people. He was a Baptist minister. That's an interesting story in itself.

WB: When did you move from the Bronx to El Barrio?

EV: We moved in 1952. We were in the Bronx roughly three years.

WB: From that time on you stayed mainly in El Barrio.

EV: From 1952 until 1954. In 1954, when I graduated from high school, I joined the United States Air Force.

WB: When did you start to write?

EV: As a child I wrote because my family encouraged education and artistic expression. My father did genetic experiments. In the backyard there were guinea pigs and rabbits that he raised. He introduced the Australian rabbit to Puerto Rico as a way to supplement the diet. He had carrier pigeons and communicated with many, many of his friends all over the island. He developed the *parcha,* the passion fruit. Nobody thought very much of this fruit, but he began extracting the juice from it, and now it is an industry. He would give people seeds, and people would laugh. Some of them would plant them and eventually, after drinking the juice, they said, "This is very good, very healthy." On Sundays after his morning sermon someone would come in, and he would put Vaseline all over their face. They would lie on a couch or sofa, and he would put macaronis in their nose and plaster on their face and make death masks of them. He had a collection of death masks of people of the town.

WB: When did you settle down in New York again?

EV: After two years of college in California. After I met my children's mother, I came back to New York in 1960.

WB: When did your first piece of writing get published?

EV: 1977. A short story called "Wild Horses." It was published in a magazine called *Nuestro*.

WB: You wrote so far, as far as publication is concerned, mainly in English. Is that right?

EV: Mainly in English, although I have a novel that was just rejected in Barcelona, but we're still waiting to hear from Buenos Aires and Mexico City.

WB: Was there a person who guided you on, whom you could call a mentor?

EV: No, other than the writers I read. I was very fortunate, coming home one time from the Air Force on leave. My sister and her friend had a job to do: cleaning out an estate in upstate New York. I liked my sister's girl friend, so they invented something. They told the man that somebody should do the yardwork and that their brother was very good at this. So I went up there, and in cleaning out a guesthouse on the estate I found a collection of about one thousand Pocket Books. I picked out, just on the basis of the titles and illustrations (because I didn't know the authors), all of Hemingway's work, all of Steinbeck's work, F. Scott

Fitzgerald, James M. Caine, who is overlooked as part of that generation of writers. Of course, all of William Faulkner, who is my favorite, and many other books. And I read all of them the rest of the summer. I just stayed in bed and just read. I didn't go out. I was amazed after about the fiftieth book because I could tell that there was something very special about Steinbeck and Hemingway and these people. But Faulkner was the person who drove me insane wanting to understand. I could feel the rhythm of the language of William Faulkner, and the things that he had to say were so complex and challenging. At the age of twenty, you know, I began to deal with the complexity of language and felt very childish and small about my lack in a language which wasn't even my own.

WB: What was the language of your childhood and adolescence?

EV: Spanish only until age thirteen, when we came to the U.S.

WB: In the outside world the language you used was English?

EV: Yes, English outside and Spanish at home. Once we came to the United States my parents did a very curious thing. Since they were very bright people, they insisted that my brother, my sister, and I use Spanish at home, but they spoke English, which they took great pains to learn. In 1950 my mother entered a contest at Alexander's department store: twenty-five words or less on your favorite American president. She won an eight-inch television with a magnifying glass. That was as much as the technology had developed then. It was an eight-inch screen, and you pulled out the magnifying glass, and it made it twelve inches or fourteen or sixteen inches or something like that. And there is still a picture in the family album of the television with rabbit ear antenna, and framed in the triangle of the antenna is a picture of *The Good Shepherd* rescuing a lamb, with myself next to the television set with my aunt and my mother.

WB: One of the terms that was used in the conference and that we feel is used at present and is much discussed in the U.S. is *multiculturalism*. We talk about a multicultural society inferring a harmonious society. What is your attitude and your opinion on that?

EV: I come from a Socialist tradition. Sometimes I say it too loudly, and people get too upset. They feel I am a zealot. But I come out of that tradition. My father was a Socialist. Writers and poets of his generation were Socialists and belonged to the Socialist Party in Puerto Rico before it became a tripartite party. And it has always seemed to me, even before reading Marx, because it was part of growing up, that as long as there is a tremendous amount of wealth and that wealth is controlled by a small number of people there is going to be competition at every level. In the United States it takes a form of ethnic competition, which I think is a horrible burden for a nation with the potential of the United States to have to put on its people. Competition is a healthy thing; there is no question about it. But when you begin to separate people and that separation is value-placed on whether you're a Jewish writer or a Native American writer, and the quality of the literature becomes subverted and in a way sabotaged, you are then doing a disservice to the artists and to the reader because you have to establish canons that are false ones.

WB: So you are saying the harmony implied in the term does not exist.

EV: It does not exist.

WB: Where do your loyalties lie, culturally and politically?

EV: Politically, I'm definitely for Puerto Rican independence and if Puerto Rico becomes a state of the union of the United States, I would seek citizenship elsewhere. That is how strongly I feel. I would go anywhere where I am allowed to live my remaining years with some dignity. But I would not remain a United States citizen. I would consider that a capitulation of my being. That is how strongly I feel about Puerto Rican independence. On the other hand, the only way I could live in Puerto Rico is if it was independent. I live in the United States as a counterinvasion, which is how I look at the presence of Puerto Ricans in the U.S.

WB: You know that in Puerto Rico that is a minority view. There would be a very small minority there today favoring that view.

EV: I mean among the intellectuals and artists independence

seems to be the stand. They want independence although most of the people are fearful of it.

WB: Now what about your cultural loyalties?

EV: That is a very interesting phenomenon, because I feel more tied in to the freedoms that exist in the United States; it is such an expression of independence, the kinds of artistic expression that you can find. The culture itself is a very vibrant one. Jazz to me is a music of liberation. The new things that are happening in art. The United States, because it is so large, can allow, absorb, and dilute a great deal, however, of the energy of young people and avant-garde artists. I could not hate any United States citizen simply because he is a United States citizen. The government, the policies anger me a great deal.

WB: When you think of New York, there exists a Latin tradition that is much older than most people are aware of. Could you comment on that and on how you feel living there?

EV: Well, as you are very much aware, wherever the people from the Iberian peninsula have gone, they have colonized the land. So New York is becoming a very Latin American city. Now there is an influx of illegals coming up, drifting up. In my neighborhood in East Harlem, traditionally a Puerto Rican neighborhood, there are now many, many Mexicans and Salvadorians. You now see people selling oranges, four for a dollar, peeled with that little machine that peels the oranges. And the Mexicans, of course, cut the orange in the middle. Now the Dominicans picked that up, and they cut the orange two thirds of the way. The Puerto Ricans have a little *tapita,* you know, a little conical opening so you can suck on the orange. But on every corner there are also shopping carts of flowers. This very stoic man or woman, Mexican, is sitting there for twelve, fourteen, or sixteen hours at a time when it's not raining, waiting for someone to buy a bouquet of flowers. And it just adds a tremendous humanity to a very rough neighborhood, where if those people were not on the corner, there would be quasi-criminal activity going on. But they are beginning in an interesting way to humanize the neighborhood, and I applaud this. I always talk to them. I welcome them to the neighborhood, and I tell them that they have a friend. But the rest of New York is becoming a very Latin city in music, in fashion, and in attitude, and this is due to a third generation of Puerto Ricans who are being influential in fashion and music.

WB: And in literature. Could you talk a little bit about the very alive Latin and Latin American literary presence in New York today?

EV: This is very, very true. Because people are coming to New York from all over Latin America, South and Central America. We have the Latin American Writers' Institute, and we put out a quarterly. It is expanding. It is publishing critical work and the work of the literary artists themselves. And there are many activities. Every semester there are workshops on translation, fiction, poetry, grammar. And there are presentations of books and book reviews, interviews. So we now have close to three hundred literary artists participating in those activities, a very vibrant society of Latin American writers.

WB: You would situate yourself within that context, wouldn't you? But you wouldn't want to be limited to it, is that what I gather?

EV: Let me tell you [*laughs*] from a real point of view. Politically, I am a Puerto Rican writer; there's no question about that. Because of my ties to the Spanish language I am a Latin American writer. For business or financial reasons you may call me a part of American literature. If anyone calls me a Puerto Rican–American writer, it insults me and creates headaches within this framework of reality that I've outlined for myself. Obviously, I am very fortunate to be able to be in the United States and publish my work because there are more opportunities for my work to be read, but I am part of a historical reality brought on by colonialism.

WB: Could you comment on 1992, on that commemorative date? How do you feel about it?

EV: I am a curious bird, and I don't hold a grudge for more than one or two years unless it's a really grievous injury. It would be so politically correct for me to begin talking about Columbus and the horrible thing that he did to the Taíno Indians of Puerto Rico, for example, who were wiped out totally. But somehow the lunacy of this man wanting to cross the ocean and go to the Indies and running into what he ran into is very interesting. I would have to, if not applaud it, at least use it as a metaphor for what I do—travel and venture into strange waters when I write—so even though it brought genocidal effect on the Americas, I think the influence of the American Indians on Hispanic culture has been extremely salubrious, especially in Middle America, Mexico, and places like that, where the Indian culture survived a lot more. In my country, Puerto Rico, the language is so full of Taíno voices, you know, Taíno words. But I can't get that crazy about Columbus.

WB: Let me jump to another question. How do you see your function as a writer in the society you live in?

EV: I have an extremely long view of the function of a writer. I choose not to be cynical about the function of the writer. If I became cynical about what I do, I would stop doing it and take up something having to do with firearms probably; but since I've chosen not to do that, I am a firm believer that each word of sincerity and beauty that a literary artist constructs adds to the cumulative literature of the human race and thus humanizes all of us. So all I can hope to do is add to that. Because I really believe that as long as people speak to each other and write, there's less of a chance of fights and wars. So on a very global level I see that as my function. Again, to bring back the idea of humanization, if I can find out something about myself and about the human condition that will affect even one person and change his life, I think I have done a great deal.

WB: Could you say something on the politics of publishing in the United States?

EV: The little I know of it there is no longer any interest, except in very small places, in literature per se. Book writing is still a very important part of the United States. Many thousands of books are published every year. But the major publishers are, by and large, corporations, and they have a bottom line. They're interested in how many books the author can sell. And they have advertising budgets to justify. And book reviewers will, although they don't believe so, pander to that system in the hopes that they themselves will be dealt with kindly when they have a book that is not up to snuff. So there is a tremendous hypocrisy and a tremendous corruption, in my opinion, in the book publishing industry in the States today.

WB: How does that affect particularly so-called ethnic writers?

EV: I believe that prizes are being handed out to people because of ethnic writing, because of their ethnicity rather than the quality of the book. I don't want to mention any names, but that has happened in the last three or four years.

WB: Is there something like a mainstream in American writing, or is that mythical? In other words, is the mainstream that does not really exist created by the mass media via publicity?

EV: There was a young man at this conference who asked a very pointed question. His concern was that literature no longer had the power to influence people. To that I would say that up until the sixties, when the American society exploded and many different countercultural forces came into play, literature had a mainstream that was very important. Today, I can't really say that is the case because that young man is right. Literature does not have the influence that television, film, and rock music have on the consciousness of the people. So to talk about American mainstream literature is an extremely confusing subject. I wouldn't want to comment on that.

WB: When you think of the Puerto Rican writers living in New York, do you see a generational change in their outlook on literature, in their use of literature, in their topics?

EV: I was at a conference recently, a conference of Hispanic writers. Chicanos, Cuban-Americans, Dominicans, Puerto Ricans, all of them write in English. And Virgil Suarez, a Cuban-American writer, put out a sheet, and on it there were twenty-five books of fiction by Cuban-American writers, post-Castro, which meant that these young people had come here in their early years and had grown up in the United States, one of them being

Christina Garcia, who has just published *Dreaming in Cuban,* and so on. I had to speak later on in the afternoon, and I began making a list of books, a bibliography of fiction by Puerto Ricans who had come here (to the United States) in their teens, when they were twelve or thirteen. And there were basically thirty-eight books of fiction by Puerto Ricans, about eight of them self-published, vanity press. So we don't have that much of an output. Now there are some new writers—I can't say they are all young—and they're all writing fiction, but I don't believe they're dealing with anything other than what was always dealt with, which was the question of ghetto conditions, ethnicity, and the terrible struggle it is to be a Puerto Rican in a closed society. I don't think there is anybody that would step forward, for example, other than Edwin Torres, who wrote three very popular books, among them *Q. & A.* and *After Hours. Q. & A.,* in particular, was like a detective novel. I don't think anybody has stepped out from under the shadow of the ghetto yet. I hope to deal with that in my next book, to use a wider canvas to paint a mosaic of the United States. The only new writer coming up now—his first book is going to be out in the fall—is Abraham Rodriguez, Jr., and his book, *The Boy without a Flag: Tales from the South Bronx,* is very good in my opinion. But it must be honestly said that the subject matter is the same. And of course, you can't fault the writer because that is where he comes from, and it is his own experience he is writing out of. I suppose that when people start going to Ivy League schools and begin living in Greenwich, Connecticut, they can write like John Updike and Cheever, but right now they are coming out of the ghetto in the South Bronx. Rodriguez writes very well. Stylistically I think he's doing something quite remarkable.

WB: What do you think of the term *Hispanic* that is used by the government, by the media, by publishers and universities?

EV: It's like *Native American,* of course. The term *Afro-American* you can understand because the tribal relationship of the black in the United States was destroyed by slavery. In the case of Native Americans it has almost been destroyed. In the case of us, the Latin people, the people of the Americas, it can't be destroyed because we are dealing with countries. We're dealing with Venezuela, Colombia, et cetera. But again it is that xenophobia, the fear of difference in the United States, the need to homogenize the experience that leads to the terms. *Hispanic* has the feeling for the media of Spain, romantic and safe. *Latino* is ghetto and dangerous, which in many respects, certainly culturally, we are.

WB: That is part of the official dogma.

EV: That's right. So it is much easier for the media in the United States to make an agglomeration of people who even linguistically are very distinct. So for the United States to try to homogenize that means showing partiality, of course. We are so individualistic that we maintain our Puerto Ricanness or Argentinianness.

WB: How do you evaluate the events of Los Angeles?

EV: It saddened me, but it should be, for the United States and for the people in power, a kind of reckoning about where the country is going, with slavery in the United States and racism in the United States at its core. It has to be dealt with; otherwise the country is going to destroy itself.

WB: Why do you think it didn't happen in New York where conditions are not that great either, at least in parts of New York?

EV: I thought about that a great deal. New York City, for example, has an equalizer, and it's the transportation system. People are thrown together whether they want to be or not. Los Angeles has these townships, you know. That's what it is. They have the blacks in one area . . .

WB: There are the freeways.

EV: Yes, connecting freeways to connect townships of people who are really ghettoized. In New York City, to me one of the biggest equalizers is the No. 6 train because it runs through the Bronx and East Harlem, which are predominantly Puerto Rican areas. By the time it gets to Eighty-sixth Street, where all the white people live, all the seats are taken, you know [*laughs*], and all the way down to Wall Street, all these people getting on to go to the great coffers of American industry have to stand, while these black ladies and Puerto Rican ladies going to jobs in Brooklyn for the Transit Authority get to sit down. On the way back, of course, they get the seats also, and the people who get on at Wall Street have to stand. So there is a great equality in having to be packed in a train with blacks and Hispanics and seeing that day after day very little happens. New York City has the seventeenth-highest incidence of crime of large cities in the United States. Many other cities are way ahead in crime, so the reputation New York City has is highly inflated by Hollywood and the media.

WB: If you had to describe your work, the vein in which you write, how would you go about it? How would you self-define your writing?

EV: It would be very difficult for me to do because it evolves; it has evolved quite a bit. When my last book came out, *Casualty Report,* this critic said that Ed Vega, who had been so satirical in *The Comeback* and *Mendoza's Dreams,* has gone back to something he has decried, which is traditional literature. But I had to point out to her that seven of the stories in *Casualty Report* had been published prior to the publication of *The Comeback* and *Mendoza's Dreams* and that I do all kinds of writing—one that is satirical about the United States and our people and one that is in the more tragic vein about the loss of human potential because of racism, because of classism, because of the natural oppression of the capitalist system.

WB: You said yourself that in part you are a satirical writer. What is your major technique in forging satire?

EV: [*Laughs.*] All I need to see is pomposity in high places for something to go off. I just finished writing a column coming out next week in *Latino News* about Quayle. I get strong feelings when it has to do with the pomposity of power. I think it's probably something that I suffer from sometimes and become pompous too. [*Laughs.*]

WB: In your novel *The Comeback* you had, among many other things, developed the idea that a Puerto Rican can actually be everything. You sort of resisted the idea that he can be limited, described, confined ethnically, circumscribed; he can be everything and be everywhere. Now, that to me is a very appealing idea. Could you elaborate on that?

EV: Well, I really feel it is not our century yet, not our decade. The nineties is supposed to be the decade of the Hispanics. I suppose that around 2030 we'll have the decade of the Puerto Ricans. At some point the world is going to really recognize what Puerto Rico represents. Puerto Rico represents a people who can adapt themselves under the most trying circumstances. Not to take anything away from other ethnic groups, but ours is a very, very flexible culture that adapts itself. Puerto Rican people marry everybody. But we take everybody in, and everybody becomes Puerto Rican. So being Puerto Rican is a state of mind. And because of it I wrote *The Comeback* to illustrate the humanity of the Puerto Rican. Even this guy who has totally lost his identity eventually was able to recoup it.

WB: In *Casualty Report* you present in the title story a veteran who has been severely wounded and who in turn will wound someone else. Could you comment on that chain of violence?

EV: I have a violent temper. I can lose my temper. I can cause physical damage. Because of this I constantly find ways to keep it in check. And verbally I am very violent. I have friends who are in the struggle, who are in jail, who are in exile, whom I admire for their humanity. Perhaps I would not do what they have done, and I can't because I don't believe in taking human life, but I can neither reject them as a way of struggle because it is the sincerity of the people that counts. And I cannot say they are terrorists, and I cannot say of them that they are less human because of their belief. I myself cannot participate, but I cannot criticize them for their sincerity. And consequently, I wrote the story in retrospect, thinking about it. The fact that the veteran had lost his foot is a way of saying how wounded we are as a people and that this one man who represents the people, the Puerto Ricans who struggle in that way and have been put into a corner, can no longer do anything but take this kind of action. If I don't have the resources or have made a conscious choice to be nonviolent, the least thing I can do is to write. If I got to the point where I felt my writing could no longer deal with my rage, then I would have to perhaps join them. As long as I have the writing, I can sublimate that great rage and anger that I feel toward the United States government and how it colonized and kept us in bondage all these years.

WB: Well, the United States has also developed things in Puerto Rico.

EV: They have developed things but at the cost of the loss of dignity.

WB: You know, the Spaniards did not have one public school—not one—when the Americans came.

EV: The U.S. didn't give a damn about the island either. They created a market for American goods. The fact is that Puerto Rico is the tenth-largest importer of American goods in the world, and for every dollar that is paid in wages to the Puerto Rican people six are taken out. That is pretty significant to me of the great rape of a basically kind and generous and, in a way, innocent people. So these young men and women who struggle using any means necessary, including violent means, I cannot fault them.

WB: Let us return to your work. In your first story of *Mendoza's Dreams* you satirize groups of people—the book industry, a public that virtually forces a writer to do things that he has done already. In which spirit did you write that? Is that a satire of what certain people expect from a writer or of what writers think they are or should be?

EV: No, I think when Claude Brown wrote *Manchild in the Promised Land* and that was followed up by Piri Thomas's *Down These Mean Streets,* it set in motion a kind of image in the American publishing industry's eye of what the Puerto Ricans were about. And consequently all that is expected of us is a testimonial literature of ghetto dimensions, which is very limiting literature, and I wanted to take a poke at that. I wanted to, at least for the sake of history, have it be said when the book was published in 1987 that somebody was thinking beyond that and somebody had become aware that they were a smart monkey, which is all that human beings are. When you become aware that you're a monkey, you have taken a step forward in your humanization. I was saying I am aware of the risk I am taking in writing, but I refuse to sell my soul to you. I want to retain my independence as long as I can.

WB: In the story "The Conquest of Fructífera Soto," which has caused some raised eyebrows, you use a whole series of paradigms and models, and you pervert those, so to speak: the immigrant story, the success story, the *crónicas.* I assume you were very conscious of doing that.

EV: Absolutely.

WB: You are using models and deconstructing them. I always find that many things that happen in Puerto Rican culture and in political life correspond to that. To me it is a very Caribbean thing as well. They send you something; you are accepting it, you are using it, but you change it around. That is what I call creolization, especially in Caribbean culture. Anything imported is there, but it is not the same anymore. And you're doing the same with many things here, with texts.

EV: The primary thing of the story was poking fun, believe it or not, at the whole García Márquez industry. And of course Mendoza claims to be a good friend of García Márquez and says that he hopes García Márquez doesn't get insulted because a character—a true person—had this monstrous penis. He hopes he doesn't feel threatened by finding out it's larger than García Márquez's character's. So I am saying, perhaps badly, there are other writers of equal courage and verve. And although I admire García Márquez a great deal, both for his political stance and for his writing, in a way, you know, it has created the same capitalistic, anti-Socialist dilemma because he is paid a great deal of money for his work; while there are other writers of as much importance, and I have to say that in spite of his great accomplishments, who go unnoticed even in his own country.

WB: I liked "Mercury Gómez" a lot, too. It is a story in which street wisdom is revealed as beating the system. It is, of course, again the turning around of a success myth. How do you see within Puerto Rican culture and writing the issue of race? It is not as obvious as in many other cultures, but it is not absent either.

EV: Race to me used to be an obsession, and at some point the love that I was given by my father's side of the family kicked in in spite of the racism and in spite of the tremendous machinery of rejection that exists in the United States about blacks. My father was a lovely man, a very bright and gentle man with insecurities that had to do with race. My father was a mulatto, a handsome, green-eyed mulatto. Finally, twelve years ago, I began recollecting my early childhood and recalled going with him on his horse, traveling to the next town and going to his aunt's restaurant. His aunt was Clemencia Montañez, the mother of a very famous Puerto Rican fighter, light heavyweight, Pedro Montañez, who fought Georges Carpentier, who was champion at that time in the thirties and forties. But going to a restaurant and seeing the dignity—this was a woman the color of ebony—the dignity of this woman who ran this tremendously successful restaurant with her son's trophies and the pictures of his accomplishments—the dignity she had as a woman, and being embraced and being doted on and being pampered in this way! Finally, those experiences kicked in, and I was able to accept the tremendous love and contribution of these people who are my relatives and who, for a time, I rejected and hid behind being Puerto Rican. The reason we can maintain our identity in New York as Puerto Ricans, in a way, is because we do not have to choose to be black or white, which is one of the demands the United States places on us. But when that kicked in, it just freed me so much from all the constraints of color so that I am at home with Afro-American culture, and I can really feel proud of the Afro-Caribbean tradition that I carry.

WB: Were you ever tempted to write poetry?

EV: I have some poems, but they are very bad, and my strongest suit, I have been told, is poetic prose. For me poetry is the highest and the most difficult standard of literature, so perhaps in old age, when I have exhausted myself and have learned the language and have had enough experience in life, maybe I will write poetry.

WB: Could you reveal the topic of your new novel?

EV: The new novel is a very broad canvas of American life. It deals with a young man, Billy Farrell, who is a genius at the jazz piano. He is a white young man who has lost his Irish-American father and is a product of Irish-American and southern white living in New York. I am attempting something which is actually extremely difficult, which is a woman's book. And I have voices, Afro-American voices, southern white voices, Puerto Rican voices, Native American voices. It's a multicultural attempt in a very humble way to begin healing the people in the United States, for whom I do not have any hate but a great love and wish that, as magnanimous as the country can be, it can finally become mature and accept all of its people.

WB: You were mentioning a while ago that you had very many literary projects going. How do you feel about completing all these plans?

EV: [*Laughs.*] Honestly, if I didn't get another idea I could easily spend the next twenty-five years completing and editing and polishing the many different novels that I have in states of incompletion. At this point there are eighteen. Four of them are finished and unpublished because in a way they are minor works, attempts I have made at different things. But of the other ones, four are so important, and I feel sometimes like I won't be able to finish them. I would love to live another thirty years. I don't like to use the word *death* because that is obvious, but the fragility of being a human mortal—you know that death can come any time—creates both a great impetus to work and at the same time a deterrent to freedom. So I am struggling with that right now. I am trying to manage that, and I am being very honest because if I do not, I think the avoidance of death accelerates the process. I struggle with it.

EIGHT

GERALD VIZENOR

interviewed by Helmbrecht Breinig and Klaus Lösch

Gerald Vizenor, born in 1934, is a member of the Minnesota Chippewa tribe. He is presently teaching as a professor of Native American literature in the Ethnic Studies Department of the University of California, Berkeley. The range of Gerald Vizenor's literary achievements is extremely broad. He has written not only books on the history of his tribe—among these The People Named the Chippewa *(1984)—but also works of narrative fiction, literary criticism, and many collections of poetry, among these, several volumes of Haiku poems. His fifth novel,* Dead Voices: Natural Agonies in the New World, *was published in 1992. For his script of the movie* Harold of Orange, *Gerald Vizenor received the Film-in-the-Cities National Screenwriting Award. The film itself received the award of Best Film at the San Francisco American Indian Film Festival. Gerald Vizenor's autobiography,* Interior Landscapes: Autobiographical Myths and Metaphors, *was published in 1990.*

In his narrative fiction, Gerald Vizenor deals above all with a variety of aspects of Native American existence between the reservation and the city. Narrative irony and the dissolution of traditional genre conventions in his works have earned him the reputation of being the most postmodern among contemporary Native American writers.

KL: To begin with, let me ask you some sort of standard question. How would you define yourself as a writer? Do you feel primarily an ethnic writer, a North American writer, an American writer, or an universal or cosmopolitan writer?

GV: There are overlapping categories of any identity, and some of them are contradictory. If I could touch on the contradiction first: Trying to reimagine a cultural voice, a tribal consciousness, a connection in my life to the imagination and the experiences in the past, to give myself and that past some meaning surely makes me, proudly in fact, a Native American Indian writer. But if I were to choose politically a category of identity as a writer I would choose an international, postcolonial literary consciousness. And I say that politically because I think that contemporary Native American writers, even traditional writers, even the traditional storytellers, have more in common with postcolonial literary experience than with American literature. That's because there is still an interest in creating a new canon, you know, a new definition of American literature. And I think Native American writers have much more in common and can benefit more intellectually, emotionally, and politically by identifying on an international, postcolonial literary experience, as there isn't any canon there yet. I assume the end of colonialism; otherwise we are talking paracolonial.

KL: I think we will come back to the question of identity later. Let me first ask a question referring to the function of literature according to your opinion. In an interview published in *MELUS* in 1981 you said that you want to educate your readers.

GV: Yeah.

KL: Do you think that satirical indirectness can meet these didactic intentions, or are you running the risk of being misunderstood?

GV: Oh, no matter what I did, I would run the risk of being

misunderstood. Simply, I'll make it more complex, but *simply* I would be misunderstood because I would feel inadequate if I satisfied a bourgeois consumer literary market. Mythic satire is indirect. I would feel inadequate otherwise. I have no interest in writing to that consumer interest. So there are two ways that I feel I must educate readers. One is that I try to discover and express in written form what I feel is closer to a literary consciousness of an oral culture, the shadows of a tribal worldview. Now, that can't be done—oral to written—but I make an effort to draw some philosophical values and perceptions of experience, differences in worldview, into writing. For one thing, just one example is motivation. It's a Western literary preoccupation for bourgeois markets that characters must be developed descriptively in such a way that they fit into a recognizable social, cultural class. And then they must be motivated in some way for the comforts of the reader to identify and then realize the experience or be trapped in the experience. Native American stories, for the most part, didn't develop characters and didn't have to motivate them. The action alone was enough to give meaning to the story. I try to play part of that, as if there were oral shadows in the silence of the written moral. Now, in written form that appears sometimes to be episodic and disconnected or a contradiction, or someone would say, "Why do I care about this character?" My interest is not that people care so much about the class definitions of the character but that they care about the action and the experiences that result from such action. Or the contradictions that arise from it.

So that's part of what I think is an "education," and then the second part is "misunderstood." I don't know about that. I can't anticipate who an audience might be and what an audience will take pleasure in. I can say that one of the most difficult books I wrote, *Bearheart,* has this constant and rather steady sort of underground readership. Now, I take real pleasure in that, and none among those readers has said to me they don't understand. So the people who tell me they don't understand—if they do, and not many people do—are looking for escape literature; they're looking for a formula literature. This is exactly I think why—this is not a fault—but this is exactly why Tony Hillerman is so popular, you know, even with many Native Americans. He's not particularly an artistic writer; he's a skilled formula writer. And he has a very interesting theme, and he develops the characters, develops the scenes, motivates people, and then resolves it. And it's a very nice genre: escape literature mystery. It's perfectly set up for film. I suppose I could go on to say why would someone bother writing literature if it's so much like film. Why not just write the film? Anyway, I don't think my books could even end up in films. So I can take pleasure in that whatever it is I choose to do in imagination is in the language game, and it's not in the play of icons, which is part of filmmaking.

HB: Would you accept Bakhtin's term of the carnevalesque for your kind of writing?

GV: I do in a couple of ways. I don't write into that because I have never taken any literary theory to write into it. But I am pleased by people who critically interpret certain scenes and episodes in my work, using Bakhtin's carnevalesque interpretations and theories. I think particularly of *Griever.* There are a number of scenes, I have read, that have impressed interpreters. The difference is this, that Bakhtin is focusing primarily upon the function of deconstructive carnival energy. But it's a political function that's allowed, tolerated by the state, and that exists in literature in a similar way. My view is that life itself is a carnival, and it doesn't seek the approval of anyone, so there's a difference there. And I say that much about the trickster stories—that there is an imaginative pleasure in these stories, and it's not a political function that allows people to escape from fascist, totalitarian, or the dominant thoughts of anyone. But otherwise I like the Bakhtinean idea. It's a healthy, much healthier interpretation, let's say, than modernism—you know, where you try to define the text within itself. So the political approach is very useful, but it's limited.

KL: So you see life as a carnival. I wanted to ask you if you think that life is an ever-repeated game with the evil gambler? I came to that because I read in your autobiographical book, *Interior Landscapes,* what you wrote about your father, who was murdered: "Clement William Vizenor lost the game with the evil gambler and did not return from the cities." Is there anything true about this image, and can it be reconciled with the notion of a carnival? An ever-repeated game?

GV: Truly, my father was not able to outwit the forces of evil, and the consequences led to his own death, and I don't know all of those. [*Pause.*] I mean, whatever led to his death, it obviously wasn't a random killing. He may have had debts; he may have been a gambler—I mean a literal gambler—but he also lived the life at that time of many people—which becomes a metaphor—that during the Depression it was difficult enough in urban areas but extremely difficult on reservations. I mean there was absolutely no work and no services of any kind, so he and his brothers moved to the city to work, and that's the gamble, and he lost. He was outwitted, lost his life.

KL: I am interested in what you think the evil gambler stands for. Does he stand for the white world or dominant culture, or does he represent evil in general? That means evil as an integral part of the world and hence part of each individual?

GV: I would argue that, by way of interpretation, the image and the description of the events surrounding the image "evil gambler" or the word game, does not stand for something. That would be representational, but it *is* something, it *is* a mystery, it *is* the contradiction of life and the shadows of tribal memories. Things go wrong, and there is exploitation, dishonesty, evil acts; all of these are contradictory and within us, not outside. Evil games are imagination, not objectivism. That, I think, is a principal distinction, a primal distinction in worldview and philosophy between Western and Native American. The Western world would purge evil, the objective and external, as if evil entered the creation of the gods and my body, and I must purge it, and I must seek a priest to constantly purge from my heart and soul any evil to reach a state of grace. In a tribal worldview, it seems to me, we always have the potential for good and evil. We are good and evil; it's not outside, it's in us. And I think you find evidence in all aspects of tribal life of this sense of a restoration of balance.

Now, I don't want to overplay that because it's like the scales of justice, and that would be a binary. But there are everywhere, say in Navajo, ceremonials when someone's in trouble; whatever it is, it affects the whole world, everything. See, it's internal; it's not outside. And so many ceremonies restore a balance, and in trickster stories they're always restoring some sort of tolerance or balance.

Let me add a couple of more ideas that abstractly describe the difference between tribal and Western. One is contradiction. Only a very few ethnologists have approached this idea of contradiction. Partly, they haven't gotten very far with it because the structuralists, you know, were so persuasive [in their belief] that we are in fact more alike than different in fundamental thinking. Especially the binary structuralists, and that has for a long time been the dominant theory. It still is in many ways. But there has been some writing, some observation that tribal cultures—not just Native Americans but tribal cultures everywhere—had a capacity for contradiction. That contradictions weren't a major obstacle, that a tribal worldview could take on contradictions as a way of life. I mean, you don't have to overcome it; you don't have to purge it; it's just part of a reality. Now, part of the contradictions I am speaking of is that we are capable of good and evil. We don't know what influences come our way. Mysteries, animals, taboos, all sorts of things disrupt our internal balance of the world. Now, out there is this eminence of evil too and this evil gambler who lurks in all of us and draws our attention through animals and stories and mysteries and contradictions and lust and greed. And these stories about the evil gambler work out these contradictions, and it's usually the trickster who outwits the evil gambler. Now, these again are imaginative language games that give a kind of philosophical voice to a character in imagination that can overcome or outwit the evil gambler. The problem is that when all of these pleasures of the literary imagination in a story become representational or symbolic, then they take on political consequences and real actions, which are recorded, and then they no longer serve as an imaginative language game. Then they are represented, then they are established externally, and then they are no longer play. I think that's one of the outstanding, in fact brilliant literary achievements of tribal storytellers, that they have not sought to represent this language game and this figurative character, the trickster, and also the evil gambler, or the ice woman or other figures in other cultures who are constantly a part of language play. You can't find them anywhere, and they exist in other cultures too, although they may take on representative forms. They are figurative, but some people actually believe they are represented in a way. So it's not just tribal cultures but others.

And it turns out that practically every culture except Western has a well-developed trickster figure in imagination. Especially oral cultures. Something happens in written form, and cultures move from oral to writing; and when they do, it, of course, becomes representational, and anthropologists have burdened us with representational definitions of tricksters. Now, what I'm trying to do is restore the play and pleasure of an imaginative figure that is transformational, which is a contradiction, which is not a developed character because it isn't representational. The trickster is a character who acts rather than poses. Such characters are eminently familiar to tribal storytellers. They don't, you know, they don't need coaching or advice.

HB: Do you see a development in your own use of what you have called trickster discourse from a more person-oriented use in your earlier texts to a more general use, where the tricksters become just a stimulus to the imagination, an element that just flits through the verbal interspace?

GV: I don't think so. Maybe the opposite. [*Laughs.*] *The Trickster of Liberty.* What I try to do is demonstrate between the stories a whole family of trickster figuration. I represent them as contradictions, mythic reversals; for instance, a Catholic nun, a Catholic priest, an entrepreneur, you know, graduates of the darkness. I mean, I gave them what conventional fiction writers would consider character description—a class, a presence, a gesture, a pose, something recognizable as representation in a contemporary world. But of course, that's anything but who they are. And then

I just deconstruct that. For one thing, they all transform, constantly in a state of contradiction. Whatever is expected of them they are not. I suppose I could play on that even on another level and say, is that any different in real life? If we touch on people's imagination rather than their public pose, we know that we all live in a *constant* state of contradiction. The very instant we smile and pose and accept the manners and gestures of someone, we might be thinking the absolute opposite, you know. I mean it's hard to put this all together. But in *The Trickster of Liberty* I set what appeared to be representational characters but are not.

HB: Well, I was thinking more of *Dead Voices*.

GV: Oh. Well, *Dead Voices* follows . . . I started with this representation in humans in *Trickster of Liberty*; they're all doing human active things, some of them quite miraculously but not miracles. I mean, ecstatic states that influence other people, material culture, animals, behavior, and all my characters have a transformational connection with animals, especially mongrels or dogs, dogs, dogs and bears. In *Dead Voices,* I take trickster stories to the city and create the ultimate contradiction that the city, which is seen as the end of stories, is actually a sanctuary. And then I play out the idea of transformation and different life forms. Well, what I was concerned about was that if I did this in a so-called wilderness area where a character sought these transformational connections I would be revisionist and romantic, and that just isn't dealing with the contradictions at hand in our own experience. So I take this woman to the city, and *there,* in the contradiction of an urban life and massive distractions, she transforms and takes on the identities of various life forms, right in town, and says there are more bears at tables in restaurants in the cities than there are in the wilderness—I mean by transformation and imagination. So your question was "Are the characters more dissociated from that original idea?" Actually, I think it's the reverse, that I'm actually strengthening this power of transformation in my characters.

HB: I was also thinking of, say, the different use of the bear concept. At the end of *Bearheart,* Proude changes into a bear and moves on to a different world, whereas in *Dead Voices* [GV: They're right there] the bear is right there, and it's in the mirror, so in a way it is also a projection [GV: Oh, I see, I see]. Thus there is a slightly more traditional aspect in *Bearheart,* whereas the handling of the concept is very contemporary in *Dead Voices.*

GV: Yeah, you're quite right. And with the mirror I'm working on image, icon, reflection, mask, and only through the mask can we discover anything and maybe nothing. It's a playing on multiple images, and it is a device to break down the romantic expectation of the real representation of the bear, that fact that the bear is in her and she's not in a traditional time, place, or environment of any kind; and the bear is in memory and imagination. So to have the mirror contain, not reflect, the bear she can't even see clearly in herself was a literary device to bring it alive because she was the only one who could see the bear. Nobody else could see that, although the anthropologists had a glimpse.

KL: Talking about masks, what do you think of the Western concept of personal identity as contrasted to group identity or tribal identity?

GV: There is certainly a lot written on that, in so many philosophical and critical contexts. The mask beneath which there is nothing is a terrifying literary and political idea, and in drama and poetry masks are, of course, necessary and important. I mean, one of those characters in *Bearheart,* the priest, has multiple masks because the priest deals in masks. I mean the whole church is a mask, nations, states are masks, political processes are masks. Some masks are more favorable than others, and we prefer to identify with them and play behind them in a way that wouldn't be tolerable in other situations. I suppose we could say that German unification is a kind of mask, isn't it? I mean it hardly works, and beneath the mask is this irreconcilable contradiction right now over abortion. It's on a political level, bears the masks of unification and a new nation after the consequences of extremely violent politics.

Anyway, in tribal cultures it's the same. A mask of Western civilization and its contradictions, a mask of Indianness, and a mask to live more comfortable in a world that expects so much from the Indian mask, that has actually been created for the individual. I probably work more with simulations than anything, the consequences of stepping out, destroying, contradicting, outwitting the expectations, the mask that's been created for Native Americans. It's easy now. It wasn't so easy in my father's generation. Most, many Indians trying to find jobs in cities couldn't get jobs as Indians. They weren't seen as good workers. In fact, my father and his brothers chose other identities because they were told that Indians don't live in houses so they wouldn't know how to paint them. So they tried other identities, Greek, Italian, and that was okay because Greeks and Italians knew how to paint things. So they got hired, and once they were successful at house painting they told the employer that, in fact, they were Indians, and he wouldn't believe them because he was absolutely convinced that Indians couldn't do this kind of work. But there, you know, you can see masks operating in a negative way, and if you make it a positive choice, and an act of survival, you can outwit even the most difficult masks imposed on you. But now it's a very positive one. It's highly romanticized, and the expectations among environmentalists, naturalists, tribal revisionists, you know—it's a very positive mask that's created for American Indians for the most part. Certainly in Europe and in large parts of the United States. That's changing, of course. Casinos have changed the mask, or casinos will end the romantic mask for quite a while. Is that what you were getting at, living into masks and contradictions?

KL: I was aiming at the question if you believe that there is something at the core of a person that doesn't change with all these roles or masks he takes on during his life.

GV: Well, your question is "Is identity essentialist?" I once had a loving friendship with a film and stage actor, and she had what I thought was a rather affected gesture with her hand just over her heart, this little turn of her hand in this affected way. And it irritated me. And I was about to be abrupt and say something because it was a pose, a mask, a gesture that was irritating, and it was a class-conscious pose. And I was about to say something when she showed me a family photograph album, and there was a picture of her about one year old, sitting on a beach, and she had that very gesture. And I realized that this was inherited in some mysterious essential way, that this gesture came with this human being into the world. So I've noticed that in many people, and obviously, tribal consciousness is inherited as gestures and shadows.

Politically, I argue against essentialism because it's too easy to define who and what we are. I argue against it because we can only discover our experience through action, through contradiction, through anarchy, and we even have to attempt to overturn our own pleasures of essential identity. Now, on the other hand, we may realize that so much of who and what we are is genetic. So that would assume a kind of biological scientism or essentialism. I touch on this quite a bit at the end of *The Heirs of Columbus*. In a way it's a very dangerous section in the book, you know. I mean I'm actually talking about the possibility of altering genetic material in such a way that people can be improved, which is really dangerous. The way I talk about it in the book is life-giving, healing, but obviously the political consequences of this are incredible. But there's no way to stop that; that's happening, that's going on. But anyway, in imagination we are essential. We discover deep intimacies of experience. We give, each of us gives meaning to our experience and shadows in a kind of essential way, and that's not always communal. And at the same time we learn things that are of great value communally, and we take pleasure from those past experiences that are represented by cultures and traditions, and some of those contradictions that arise from them.

For example, I try to divide, for purposes of discussion, all experience and identity, but particularly tribal experience and identity, in three ways. First there is an intimacy, at once an emotional dream language. That knowledge in dream is so intimate that we seldom share that with anyone. Occasionally, we come in contact with people with whom we feel this mysterious bond, and we can communicate that understanding, usually in love relationships. Sometimes we're wrong about that, and we pay a terrible price. Then there's privacy. Privacy is determined largely by social and cultural values. Some cultures, nations, are less private than others. Americans seem to be willing to talk about anything: sex life, family, everything. They gossip about everything. British tend to be more restrained about family business. Germans are quite protective about privacy, especially in matters of public discourse, newspapers, access of writers, photographers and things like that, with very developed laws about privacy. But each culture, each tradition has different values, and among tribal cultures there are differences about what might be thought of as private. Now, that's not what's intimate. We all know what's intimate. What we aren't sure about is what's private and public. That varies.

Now, the reason I'm pointing this out is that forever the conquerors assumed the right to whatever was private and transformed that into their public, and they also assumed access to the intimate. Ethnologists, anthropologists believed that it was their right to enter the intimate, to discover the tribal, the sacred, and intimate. And when I talk to students about this, I say, "Would you tolerate in your own family any of the experiences of Indians?" Of course not; they wouldn't. They wouldn't want some anthropologist hanging around trying to find out what the meaning of their meals was, or sexual practices, or the function of their material culture, or their dreams and myths. I mean, this access is assumed as a kind of right of the social sciences, and that raises questions about what is essential too. And also what's public and private and what is communal. Now, here are some contradictions that are not easily understood, and they are differences in worldview. It's said of Indians, because the people who have studied them say this, that many Indian people walk into the public masks and take comfort in them because it's an easy way to be understood. And I don't want to do that. I want to disrupt that. I don't want to be easily understood. I want to complicate the tribal world.

I want to point out just a couple of things about these contradictions of the public, private, and intimate. The general view is that Indians are communal, and the Western world is individualistic and usually material, right? This is a comfortable distinction to make. People take instruction from that, I mean, life value. And yet here's the contradiction. Indians, tribal people, are more individualistic than contemporary whites. And here's what I mean by that contradiction. Just a couple of examples. Tribal people know each other usually through nicknames and the stories behind each nickname. The tribes did not have a surname system. So behind each nickname is a story, and in a lifetime you could have many nicknames, depending upon experiences and how people saw you and what you did. Highly individualistic, isn't it? Not only a nickname that distinguishes an individual absolutely from anybody else but a story that's so unique that it gives you identity. Very individualistic. There's hardly any of that remaining in American popular culture. Hardly any of that remains. People want to dress alike; they want to consume something that will make them look like they're not individuals. Another contradiction is this idea that so many interpreters of Indian life story and autobiography have, and that is that Indians are communal, that they couldn't write autobiography because it's antithetical to their very being of essential communal experience. Now, what rubbish! I mean it seems to me the opposite is true. It's Americans, European Americans who have nothing to write about; they don't have any individual experience, and it would seem to me they are incapable of *auto*biography.

Just one more example. In most tribal cultures there are vision quests. Many individuals do this, and they do this in extreme conditions. They detach, meditate, concentrate, and wait in deprivation to be visited by some force or mysterious energy that exists in the world through animals, through trees, through some life form that becomes an extraordinarily unique experience. So unique that no one else has it. No one else has it. Such as a voice and a story that connects you to some absolutely intimate, sacred memory. Now, what could be more highly individualistic than that? There's nothing like that remaining in Western civilization.

There's nothing in the church except the possibility that some people have ecstatic communion with their creator. Now, the unique thing about this is that nicknames, vision quests, which are extremely individualistic, are *not* separations from communal life. Someone who goes on a vision quest knows that the community he comes from supports this, hopes that it will work out; and if and when it does, the experience and stories may benefit the community. So this extreme individualism is a part of the community. It gives the community energy, power, healing power, insights that it can share collectively. I am generalizing this almost in an idealistic way. Now, in contemporary American society primary experience of individualism is in consumerism. Well, that's hardly individualistic, and you don't have anything when objects are lost. You don't even have community, much less individual identity. So these contradictions, and it seems to me that there's a longing in the Western world that is realized on a literary level in the discovery of tribal cultures. In other words, it's a complete projection: what's missing is found in the other, especially if the other has been conquered, colonized, and yet remains in some way unique, different, and mysterious.

HB: Let me pick up the term "tribal," which you have just mentioned. You prefer it over "Native American" or "American Indian," but the term in itself seems to include both the communal and the private in such a way that it seems possible to apply it to other groups as well and other ethnicities. Is America possibly turning multitribal?

GV: That's a way to affiliate and feel comfortable and also to feel cared for in a way, you know, that you have some ultimate security, that you know you have some tribal support. I use the word to avoid, as often as possible, "Indian," which, of course, is totally unacceptable, and it's a risk because of the problems of language, the changes in language value. The word *tribal* doesn't work in discussing African cultures because it could be seen more often as pejorative than postmodern. It suggests something primitive, and I wouldn't use that word anywhere else in the world. But I think America has a positive association with the word *tri-*

bal, and it's at least not pejorative in its current use. So it serves me, this general value in the word world of the communal. It's not easily defined, but it suggests something other than material, other than consumer culture, that it's tribal in the sense of Indian, that it's shared responsibilities and things like that. So then I can specify what I mean by it and not have to deconstruct it. It comes into the language right now. It may well change. Probably after a decade or two of fascist tribal groups—you know, skinheads and clans and white supremacists in America and things like that—it will probably be exhausted as a useful word, so I'll have to come up with something else.

HB: Let me come back to the question of identity. Last night we talked about Diane Glancy, who calls herself a Cherokee with one-eighth Cherokee blood, and, say, Ishmael Reed, who also has about that proportion of [GV: Indian, Irish, Black] Indian blood but of course chooses to affiliate himself with African-American culture. So has cultural affiliation become a matter of choice?

GV: Can't do a yes or no on that. Is cultural affiliation a matter of choice? It's a matter of responsibility, and people do make choices that are responsible to communities. The identity question is so complex that the background conversation we'd have to do to get at it would take the rest of the day. But let me touch on one of the great burdens: the problem of mixed blood. Everybody's been mixed forever. So that's not new. What I'm trying to argue is that mixed-bloods are not incomplete. They're not half of something, or this or that. They're whole people. Now that's difficult in America and in the world because the world is not very tolerant of the idea that someone who is mixed is a whole person. The idea is that mixing is less of something and—depending upon the values in a nation—usually the best part, in the context of racialism, is white.

Now, in America it's an irony. Because of the interest in assimilation, the public policies of assimilation, Indians seem to become white with intermarriage. African-Americans, however, always stay African. They don't become white because of a different sense of racial privilege and an idea of assimilation. Also, Americans don't, and Germans as well, pretend to be African. But Germans and Americans have made an industry out of pretending to be Indian. Now, it's a serious complication and contradiction that, on the one hand, we have—just these two countries for the moment, Germany and America—invested an enormous amount of personal energy and wealth into the invention and pretension of being Indian. At the same time, both countries have a critical consciousness about who is an Indian and who is not, and they make general negative categorical comments about the mixed-blood. They prefer the pure. I'm not playing on any historical revision here because Americans do the same thing. And it's such a difficult condition of identity because that kind of language leaves someone who's mixed-blood feeling a sense of inadequacy, that in fact the pretend identity is more significant than the mixed identity, which is real. So all of these questions. And then the federal government should establish this racist categorization of blood quantum as if such a thing were possible. If they choose a language of genetic influence or appearance or something, at least that would have a play that could be realized in genetic theory. But blood quantum, as if identity is by a volume!

So that's what Diane Glancy has to deal with and every mixed-blood has to deal with. The reality is that Indians have been mixing forever. Sometimes friendly and sometimes not. And in my part of the country, the mix is primarily French because of the fur trade. And British. In the Pacific Northwest, Russian and English. In the Southwest, Spanish mixed-bloods. So there is intermarriage everywhere, and everyone is mixed in an immigrant nation. But these racial categories obligate people to see themselves in a certain way. Now, my view is this: that identity is a choice, but identity is a responsibility. And it's not who people are by their fractions or their quantum; it's who people are by their responsibility with peers and families and communities. Now, I don't mean you have to be agreeable, but you have to be responsible. So I find it interesting, for example, that very few, or hardly any, of the contemporary writers, Indian writers right now, have ever been active in communities. No radical work, no community organization. Now, I don't want to bring false credit to myself here, but I have been, and I take some personal pride in having argued in streets and communities the very difficult issues of identity and medical care and education and those matters. For a long time I've taken radical positions. I've paid certain prices, you know, of admission to experience. And I believe in that; I believe experience has to be almost radically acted and earned to be responsible. That doesn't make anybody any better than anybody else. It's a difference that exists, and I think you can see it in literature.

Charles Larson, you know, when he wrote that book *American Indian Fiction*—terrible book, but it was the very first book, published in the seventies, very first study of American Indian fiction; sadly, the second one was the best because Larson was so poorly organized and his categories were stupid—he faced an interesting problem: how do you decide who is an Indian writer? You can't, he pointed out, go by blood quantum because even though someone claims he's an Indian, you know that may just be generations away. There's no contact with it. So he settled upon an idea similar to "peer recognition." If he could discover that a writer who was identified as Indian was recognized by his or her peers, that was substantial support and validation of Indian identity. He said this because, of course, there are so many fakes who pretended to be Indian and who wrote as Indians, and that would have damaged any critical interpretation if he ended up with half a dozen people who were not Indian who claimed they were. And also those books that were "as told to," you know, someone else who helped an Indian writer. And in many cases, both people were invented. So I think some sense of responsibility and peer recognition is very important. And that means you have to earn through responsible acts the choice of identity. I mean you can choose it, but you have to choose to *do* certain things to be responsible for a community, for an idea, for memory, for something. I believe in that. I don't think it's enough to just discover that you've got Indian blood. That's interesting. It *is,* and it's a wonderful connection and start. But you have to be responsible for that. You have to be responsible for memory and history. So if you make that choice, you have to establish some responsibility by way of an act.

Now, there's a really wonderful person, Hertha Wong, who has just written a book on Indian autobiography. She is a very good scholar. In the preface to this book she speaks of herself as being Indian. She's just discovered that this book has even more meaning now because she just discovered that she's got Indian blood. I think that's really interesting, but what is she trying to say? That now, all of a sudden, this text has an essentialist meaning? It's a really interesting problem and question, and we should be suspicious of someone in a preface to a book claiming this. I'd be much more impressed if she claimed experience and responsibility for her community, for memory, history, for her people. But she can't even identify which tribe she's from. You know, this could be a visitation with essentialism. We can come back to that, that the genes may in fact in the end make the difference, right? But for our purposes in literature, community engagement, it's the choice of taking responsibility for history, for colonial circumstances, for trouble and pleasure and pain and engaging in that directly. I can even argue more strongly that if you haven't been part of community organization, if you haven't argued some issues, if you haven't taken a position in the name of history and your experience, you don't have a right to claim tribal identity or to write about it. That's pretty strong but it's important.

But then we have the other extreme. We have Jamake Highwater, who poses as an Indian without an intimate sense of responsibility for that identity. I couldn't possibly accept his books because he manipulated and falsely presented himself. Or Forrest Carter's *Education of Little Tree,* which is the most recent example of simulated identities. Carter is not known for his responsibilities in an Indian community. He's a good writer, but I was suspicious of the content because it was too linear, it was too romantic, and this is not a "true story" as the publisher claims. However, this is a useful book for critical reasons of identity. And sure enough, it turns out that he's not who he said he was; he may have Indian blood, but he was never responsible for that experience. That's important to do. Otherwise we have the worst aspect of postmodern consumerism, total simulation, and the simulation precedes the real and in fact is the real, and then the real has to compete with the lie and simulation. I said more than you asked, but then . . .

HB: Your notion of the mixed-blood, of the fruitfulness of bringing together polarities, as one might say, takes me back to a question of literary technique. Would you agree that your literature is basically metaphorical in the sense that you put in two or several semantic poles and have the imagination fill in the interspace, the dream space as you say? It's a technique, I think, that works both in your haiku poems with the different lines, with the different images, and in your fiction with longer complexes developed. It can also be found in your mixture of genres, in your bringing in nonfictional elements when you quote from criticism and so forth. Would you agree that, in the sense of Ricoeur's "creative metaphor," this is a basic principle to your writing?

GV: I do like to leave the pleasure of the meaning and interpretation to the reader, and so, rather than didactically stating or assuming the information that I've obtained, I actually lay out the images and information and leave it to. . . It is a metaphor, but I leave the ends open. What's interesting is that some readers don't believe the historical documents. They think they're fictional, but I can't account for that. I can only act responsibly in that way. It is interesting though. People have some difficulty accepting historical or other documentation in fiction, and I think it's the consumer interests of fiction that make fiction a lie, a simulated escape, you know. Of course, I see fiction as having the healing power of stories, or liberation. At least that's the way I want to write and the way I feel about literature. It has more in common with the postcolonial literature. Because I see that literature as liberation, not in a linear way, but the experiences, and much of that literature also draws upon historical documentation. And the contradictions of history in colonialism, realized as metaphors, are the characters of liberation. And I think readers can be liberated in that way too. They can be liberated from their own pretentiousness. They can be liberated from their own possession of the image, their own guilt through colonization. I take pleasure in Native Americans who find themselves in my work. And I have been greatly honored by a small number, but a very significant number, of Native Americans who write and tell me that, in fact, something in my work did liberate them, that they were not able to see themselves until they read my stories. Most often through my autobiography. And I think it's because I argue for the experience of a whole person. And yet, in the autobiography, I say nothing that's intimate. I say much that's private, a witness to the private, but you won't find confession of the intimate in my work. I believe the essential is intimate, and the intimate is mine. I write memories that are imagined, historical, and private.

KL: I wanted to ask you a question about the mixed-bloods or crossbloods, as you like to say. Do they have a chance or are they the ones capable of creating a new culture? In some sort of dialectical process between the two inherited streams of culture, a culture that will give them their own sense of place?

GV: Well, there's certainly a tension there, isn't there? I mean there's a tension of discovery and liberation, and my argument is that we become whole by this, not parts. But everyone is mixed, everyone. So everyone can discover this. People are just mixed in different ways, and the consequences and interpretations of their differences as sources of identity—let me put it another way. What difference do we make out of the differences? That's my interest. In the past the differences have been violent and terribly damaging, and I'm arguing that the differences are liberation; they're the discovery of a whole person. Throughout tribal history mixed-bloods have always been active in tribal business. I think, not now but perhaps in a decade or two, someone may be able to develop a very impressive critical interpretation about the tension of mixed identity being the source of energy among every, every contemporary Native American writer. They're all mixed-bloods. The difference is that not many of them said so in the beginning, very few. They allowed publishers to present them as the essential Indian. But every author is a crossblood, in the heart and the word. And that's important, and I wish more authors would speak of that. It's important to know. That would break down this Karl May expectation in Germany, for example. It would enrich the idea of identity. It would make it much more intriguing and interesting. And it would say much more about the world, about colonialism, about postcolonialism, about our resistance to colonialism and the literature of dominance. It would obligate people to enter this tension and imagine it and become whole themselves, you know, to see people in a different way. But by perpetuating this image of essential racial purity, and especially if someone fits the physical description of a kind of Karl May Indian, you know, in a way they're doomed to their own simulation. I mean they have to interpret the difference or argue out of it.

I started a course on "People of Mixed Descent," at Santa Cruz several years ago, and I teach it at Berkeley now. I approach the class historically and theoretically because I want it to be a serious academic seminar. With few exceptions the students who have taken it are crossbloods. Now, no one on campus thinks much about this except the people who are crossbloods. Practically every minority student is a crossblood. And yet they have to choose from just a few generic racial categories. They're very limited: African-American, Native American, Asian-American. Well, break down the Asian into a dozen or more groups. So there will be students in my classes who are Korean-Japanese. Imagine that mix! Imagine having to decide on a category that is less than a whole person; you're whole only by simulation, political simulation, and not by experience. And you have to deny something in order to be less than whole. These classes have been the most exciting, the most moving, and the most liberating of anything I've ever taught because we study the theories of race and culture, the developments of racialism in history, and some of the evil consequences of racial categorization and exclusion; then colonial contact, mixed relations, some willing, some unwilling; and then we talk about our own experience. To hear that experience and to hear people speak of themselves as a whole person instead of a fragment here and there is very rewarding. The subject has been the most encouraging because people have been so enthusiastic and so eager to take hold of this complicated idea, and there's a lot of tension but it's so liberating.

HB: I should like to wind up in a lighter vein. What is a panic hole?

GV: The experiences of a panic hole are intimate. However, it is in literature, and I have written about it, so the idea is public. That the earth must love to hear my voice. Why else would the earth have given me voice? And I take pleasure in shouting back into the earth the very tension of my existence, the very *tension* of my existence, and the earth is better for it, and so are we with the earth.

NINE

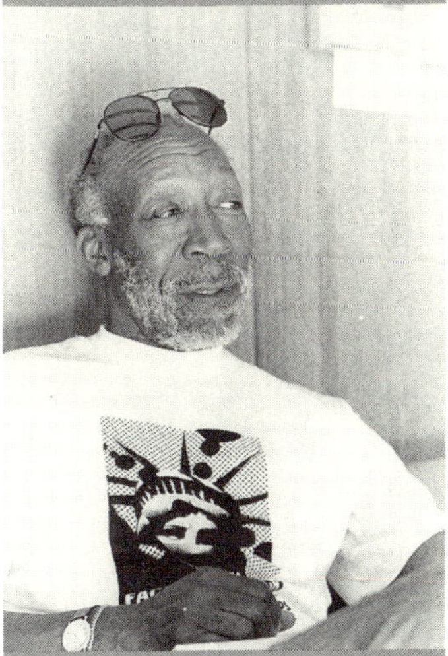

JOHN A. WILLIAMS

interviewed by Wolfgang Binder

John A. Williams was born in Jackson, Mississippi, in 1925. Today, after several guest professorships at various American universities, the novelist, dramatist, essayist, nonfiction writer, and publisher lives in New Jersey.

John A. Williams achieved fame with his novel The Man Who Cried I Am *(1967), in which the author addresses the race problem in the United States. Several other novels followed, among them* Sons of Darkness, Sons of Light *(1969) and* !Click Song *(1982). In 1983 he received the American Book Award of the Before Columbus Foundation. His work is distinguished by a rejection of the literary cliché, whereby the African-American protagonists appear as the victims of society because they do not know their own history. It is this subject—the overcoming of the past, along with the international theme and the plight of the African-American family—that are the dominant themes in both his fictional and nonfictional works. As an author, he sees the possibility of a new aesthetics for African-American literature in the mixture of history and fiction.*

WB: John, could you tell us when and where you were born?

JW: I was conceived in Syracuse, New York, because my mother had gone up there to work and met my father, whose family was up there already. And because I was the firstborn, she returned home to Mississippi, and that is where I was born and lived for the first six months of my life.

WB: So your family was actually not a southern family?

JW: Not on my father's side. If it was, we don't know. They may have preceded the Underground Railroad. They couldn't wait for it. As a matter of fact my father's family is probably in part related to the Onondaga Indians of the Iroquois Nation.

WB: What kind of a family was that? How many kids were you?

JW: Well, four of us, two boys and two girls, survived. Two died in infancy. It was a Depression time family, which meant that it was kind of tough. I was just thinking the other day about the most pleasant place we lived during childhood, and it was a giant four-family house in Syracuse, and the neighborhood was very integrated then. A Jewish family, a peddler and his daughter and son on one side, an Italian family above them, a black family upstairs over us. But the whole block was pretty much that way.

WB: When did you start writing seriously?

JW: I guess I started writing "seriously"—I'll put that in quotes—while I was in the navy, because I had such a rough time in the navy. Whatever my reaction was to the navy only got me in more trouble; so sometimes when I was in the brig I just got pencil and paper and would write down all this crap and call it poetry, which, of course, it was not. But I think that's where it started.

WB: Were books important at home?

JW: No, books were not important. As a matter of fact, reading back over Richard Wright's life in the family and his interest in the books, I think his family, like mine, essentially felt very threatened by books and my interest in them. With the exception of the Bible, books were considered to be pretty much troublemakers.

WB: And too worldly?

JW: Well, I don't know if they were too worldly or not. They may have had the sense that if this kid grows up reading books, he's got to know more than I do, and then where in hell am I going to wind up, you know?

WB: And where did you go from Syracuse?

JW: I stayed in Syracuse until 1953 or so. I had gone to the junior high school and high school, and I played on the high school football and basketball teams and ran track. Then the war came, and I went off to war from '43 to '46; I hadn't finished high school before I went into service because my parents were divorced and I helped out working. But when I got back, and the GI Bill was available, I went back and finished that last semester in high school before I started college at Syracuse. Actually I went south to start. I had gotten something, a kind of a promise of an athletic scholarship.

Anyway, so I went down there about two weeks before classes started to Morris Brown College. And if you know Morris Brown, you can imagine what it was like in 1946, and I had forgotten how bad it had been in the navy with southerners. So I guess a week before classes started I was in the train coming back north, and I just enrolled in Syracuse and finished up there, did some graduate work.

WB: Apart from your literary work you have always also been a journalist and a teacher. Could you sketch that triple career briefly?

JW: Actually, I was doing some teaching at Syracuse with labor unions. I don't know why they asked me to, but I would go and talk to these labor groups, and it may have been because I also did a lot of factory work in Syracuse. My first job when I came out of school was at the foundry, where I had worked summers. Then I also worked as a caseworker for the Welfare Department and then as a worker for the Children's Protective Service, which was a pretty grim job. Talk about children today being abused. It was just awful. And then I guess I had written for the *Post* in Syracuse and occasionally for the *Progressive Herald,* which was a black weekly. I know it sounds cliché, but I had always loved the smell of newspaper, you know, and being able to produce this stuff and to put words together to tell a story. This I was always in love with. But what I discovered was that when I was of age and had had some training to do this, doors were pretty much closed to me, although even in Syracuse I wound up as a copywriter for a white public relations agency. They were very nice guys. So I was getting all kinds of experience but not being able to really put it into practice. And then I think after I did *The Man Who Cried I Am,* I was asked to go up to City College and teach. So I said, why not? I enjoyed it immensely. I think I did two years there.

WB: Was that in '68?

JW: It would have been '68/'69. Then I was invited to teach a summer at the College of the Virgin Islands at St. Thomas. I'm saying to myself, well, hell, if it's all going to be this exotic. [*Laughs.*] So we went down there for a summer, and after that I did a year at Sarah Lawrence College. Then I was offered a CUNY Distinguished Professorship at La Guardia Community College. I think that's where I really got sucked into the whole teaching thing. Then I left there and went up to Boston, then did a summer university at the University of Hawaii as well. I was also a Regents lecturer at the UC Santa Barbara.

WB: When was that?

JW: That must have been about '74. And then we moved to New Jersey, and I got tired of beating my head against the traffic getting into Manhattan. I sort of put the word out, and then I got into Rutgers, and I've been there now for fourteen years.

WB: What do you teach there?

JW: I teach undergraduate journalism and graduate creative writing. I really have not taught literature in a number of years now.

WB: What are some of the key impressions of American students in those fields for you? Are there certain trends, group mentalities that you can decipher as being part of a racial setup or functioning on a class scale.

JW: Let's start with undergraduate journalism. On the whole, people have fallen in love with television. When they think about journalism, they think in TV terms. There are very few people who look forward to going into print. They are ill-prepared in terms of language and history, of politics, economics, all the things that you really should know. Younger journalists don't seem to be as eager today to know as much about the world as possible. What they want to know is what will get them over and that's it. In graduate writing we get a lot of people who apply, and it is my job to say yea or nay. And I like to keep the class at about ten people. That's very difficult to do. Now, as any teacher of creative writing will tell you, if you get one or two people out of three or four years you are doing pretty good. And that's about what you get. I will tell you one crucial thing that has changed for me in terms of being a teacher, and that is it seems as though all freshmen or sophomores would want to do papers on injustice. Nobody does those kinds of papers anymore. They just don't.

WB: Even though it should be obvious to them that that would be a great topic. At this conference, in the mass media, and I'm sure in the U.S., the term *multiculturalism* has been used and abused over the past few years. How do you feel about this term? Do you think it is covering up things? Do you think it describes the society and cultures in the U.S.? Do you think it is homogenizing things that are not really in harmony?

JW: Luci Tapahonso said something yesterday which I thought was quite apt. She had no qualms with the term, but she said it is this kind of study that is going to help bring her work to the fore, and to that extent it is very good whatever the title is. But titles become slogans, and slogans become clichés, and they go the way of the change in the weather. But I think at the time being we're sort of stuck with it, and most people are going to use it, and hopefully a lot of people understand what the hell it means.

But that is the problem with coming up with a heading for any kind of new venture. And by the way, it is not a terribly new venture because, as we mentioned earlier, there have been a lot of people who've been working in this area for quite a while without being labeled as multiculturalists but just people who are involved in literature.

WB: Just mention a name or two?

JW: I would say Bruce Franklin, who is my colleague at Rutgers, Jim Hatch at City College; I would say Michel Fabre, Ishmael Reed, a teacher I had at Syracuse named Dave Owen who is now dead. So there've always been teachers who have been ahead of the field in terms of decades, not just years. I haven't said a lot of the textbooks, but publishers are using those terms interchangeably—multiculturalism and diversity—and I suppose as long as they sell books they'll be happy. But I think those of us who've been involved in the field for a long time have a right to feel or to hold reservations about what these labels actually mean.

WB: Into which literary tradition would you put yourself? In which literary context do you feel at ease?

JW: I'm not sure. Certainly not all the terms that are being knocked about in postmodernism. I feel more closely related to the people in the Progressive era. I have always found that to be a very impressive period. And probably too short a period in the way we form periods in literature. And not given half enough credit.

WB: You would see the term *protest writer* as limiting you?

JW: Well, when many people use that, it is a limiting term. But I nevertheless feel that for a long time it was a label of honor.

WB: Do you feel a special closeness and a special allegiance to the so-called Third World as a black American? Is that included in your vision of things? Do you also apply your criteria to the U.S., or not?

JW: I have to admit that one of the things I have always been a sucker for is the underdog. I mean, I can watch a boxing match and see the poor guy getting beat up and say, "Come on, do something! Help yourself! Whatever!" But as soon as he starts winning, that changes. So to answer your question, yes. As long as people cannot help themselves or defend themselves or whatever, yes.

WB: Would you say that in particular it is Africa that you would relate to most intimately?

JW: It is not only Africa. It is my people in the United States and by extension other people who don't even know they're in the same situation in the U.S. and around the world.

WB: Do you think that your journalistic career has strengthened that tendency or developed it even?

JW: I don't think so.

WB: You don't think so?

JW: I don't think so, no, because the pieces that I have really wanted to do on that situation are pieces that most editors are not very interested in, and I could give more voice to that situation in fiction than I ever could in journalism.

WB: Do you see American society holding together or falling apart today?

JW: I think it is falling apart. And I am not sure what it would take to find adhesive to put it back together again. In a great part the media is to blame for that as well as the politicians. Spengler always said that the journalist just obeyed the masters. And I think a lot of philosophers and contemporary ones said essentially the same thing. But they still do it. We talk about the Watergate business and how great the press was, but actually there was only the *Washington Post* and two print reporters and CBS and a couple of broadcast reporters. And Harry Ashmore, the Pulitzer Prize winner from Atlanta, from the *Little Rock Gazette,* said that if it weren't for these four or five people we wouldn't have had Watergate.

WB: Do you feel that since Nixon, Reagan, and the Bush administration, that tendency to be separate and unequal has been enforced rather than easing up?

JW: Yes, it has been enforced in a way that's not as subtle as that. Try to explain to students that if you go to a press conference and you start asking tough and nasty questions, they're going to pull your press badge. You'll never get into another conference, you know. They know who you are. They're just going to make it damn difficult for you to get any information from the White House. And that's the game, whether it is the White House, the state house, the city hall, all in the same way.

WB: What about race relations between the different ethnic groups? Have there been changes in the '80's?

JW: Well, I think the press tells us that there've been changes and great antagonisms, and we know that the Hispanic community is growing by leaps and bounds and that it'll probably be the largest one in the country by the year 2000. That may be true between some Asian ethnics and black and Latin ethnics, but I'm not sure that the antagonisms are that deep between black and Latin because now they share so much of the same history, so much of the same blood and things of this sort, so Asians tend to be the newcomers who don't have that particular history. And in fact, they are very often placed in a position that in order to survive they must sort of economically bleed out these communities. I just find it incredible, for example, that in south central L.A. there are seven hundred liquor stores. More than any other number of liquor stores in any other community in the whole of the United States. But we've always known that in Harlem, in Southside–Westside Chicago, you find more liquor stores and churches than elsewhere in the city. But to return to those antagonisms: The individuals who understand that for anything to really work for ethnic groups there must be cohesion between them, and once that is achieved, you make your political move, and then you can divide the spoils. I mean that is what the Brahmins did when the Irish came and the Irish did when the Italians came, and on and on. So it is a pattern we have to learn to repeat. And I think the press is not our friend in this situation.

WB: How do you see the events in Los Angeles? I have the impression that the press was in part very unfair, attributing everything at first to the black community, whereas I think there were fifty percent Hispanics involved and quite a few whites in lootings, et cetera. It was a multiracial riot. Would you agree to that?

JW: Yes, I would. And I think it was very important that the press worked very hard to create the impression that it was a black revolt. For obvious reasons, because if you have all of these people in rebellion that says something very, very bad about the system. Extremely bad. But the problem with Los Angeles—I have relatives there still—is that in that particular community there are practically no services. Now this was before that happened. There were very few banks, very few supermarkets, lots of check-cashing places, little fast-food shops, lots of churches, lots of funeral parlors, lots of liquor stores. But the services you need to have a viable community just really did not exist for that large number of people. So there are a lot of antagonisms that were building up there. Not to mention the fact that the cops are always cops.

WB: So you would not say it was simply a repetition of Watts?

JW: No, I would not. No, not at all. We may get a book or two on it later on, but it is not going to be right now. A former student of mine at New York University, who works for *Esquire* in West Hollywood, came and visited a couple of weeks ago. He said he could see the fire from his apartment building. One would start here, the next one would start a bit closer to his neighborhood, a little bit closer, and he said it was just awesome. It seems they could not contain the fires. Now, in the neighborhood itself I have two sisters and a brother living. One sister is very close to USC—that area was pretty much devastated. As a matter of fact, USC was sending out notices to parents of potential students saying it is okay, it is all right, don't worry. Another sister lived a bit further to the west, toward Hollywood, and they just burned down a supermarket across the street. It was gone. There was no postal service. People had to go to the post office to pick up their mail. And since she gets a widow's pension—her husband had worked for the city—she had to go get that. My brother, who's not well, had to have friends come and get him and drive him to a market in some other neighborhood.

WB: The year 1992 is one of the big dates for commemoration and celebration. Do you have feelings about this year of Columbus as it is termed very often? Does that tempt you for a piece of journalism?

JW: Yes, it does in a way. I've been looking to see pieces on the twenty-ton Olmec heads that they've found from one side of Mexico to the other. For somebody to do a review of Alexander von Wuthenau's books, *African Faces in the New World*. All we're going to get out of this is what Columbus's journey may have done, but there are a lot of other things that could have come out of this. It is a celebration; it is not an occasion to learn anything. And celebrations engender money and that's it.

WB: So you would keep festivities low-key?

JW: I would. I would throw in as much education as I possibly could get away with, you know.

WB: You don't see that?

JW: I don't see that happening.

WB: How do you see, if that's possible at all, your function as a writer in American society? I mean both in black and white society. I hesitate to use those primitive terms, but they are very American. I prefer the concepts of culture to that of race because I think it is very demeaning. But anyway, this is couched in American language.

JW: I understand. I think my central function is to tell the truth to myself and, in extension, to my fellow human beings. And I just find the truth is so hard for people to absorb, particularly if it is an unpleasant truth. You will get—somebody mentioned that the other day—you get a lot of facts, but facts are not necessarily truth. That is basically what I see as my function: to deal with these truths and have people respond to them. At least give them alternatives so they can see that what they are living is not the truth but a lie. And I am not sure if a writer can be sure he or she is doing anything more than that.

WB: Let me ask you about the politics of American publishing, the conspiracies or just the interest.

JW: I can remember that when I first started writing there were editors who were very concerned that the work would offend the southern readers. It sounds like this was five hundred years ago or so, but it wasn't. We're talking about thirty or thirty-five years ago. The mentality of the editors—let me say that I think there were better editors then—is not, in my opinion, very high. But I was lucky enough to get one of my magazine editors who moved to books to do a couple of what I thought were important books for me. But the level of intellect in understanding the world has diminished tremendously. There has always been a sense that if you have a Richard Wright, you don't need a Ralph Ellison; if you have a Ralph Ellison, you don't need a Jimmy Baldwin; if you have a Jimmy Baldwin, you don't need an Ishmael Reed; and on and on and on. That's the one-at-a-time syndrome, which has been pretty much destroyed when it comes to black women. We have seen this repeated with Asian-American authors—the women versus the men. But those are some of the problems we have. And the hard currency issue—the purchase of American publishing companies by some of the European companies like Maxwell, Bertelsmann—they have really made the Americans start to look to the absolute bottom line. We are not talking about literature, serious literature, that makes people think about who they are, where they are going, where they came from. We are talking about writing where people get in a sack and romp, and serial killers.

WB: Sensational material?

JW: Right. So we are getting a lot of that to the detriment, I think, of a considerable number of very good writers. Then they go to the small presses if they are lucky, and because small presses don't have the money to publicize except in a general press release way, we seldom hear about them until it is too late. They become famous suddenly or they are gone suddenly. So we have a real problem, and I think it is based on the fact that nobody takes books seriously in America anymore. I do textbooks occasionally, and I have always felt like an idiot when the publisher's editor says, "Well, how are we going to structure the teacher's guide that goes with the textbook?" And I'm always thinking, a teacher needs a guide to teach this book?

WB: Do you feel that since the mid-eighties the male African-American writer has it harder than before to come to the foreground?

JW: Yes, I think it started a little bit earlier than that, but yes, generally speaking. One of the reasons may be the proliferation of women editors, but that's not necessarily the case. I think there were fewer before, and then they tended to do all kinds of books, males, females, whatever. But I think right now there are a lot of female editors who feel safer dealing with what it is they know, what it is they best know.

WB: Is there something like an American mainstream literature, or is that fictitious? Is that created by the media, by vested interests?

JW: Oh, I think it is created by vested interests, and I think the mainstream keeps changing. You could go from a WASP mainstream in which Hemingway is insulting Jews and blacks in every corner and not in the voice of the characters but in the authorial voice. And then you would move to a situation where you would get Jews at the bottom rungs of the literary establishment. And now that has changed, so a lot of Jews, not all, are at the top of establishments, and I am not sure who comes next. But we can see the ethnic changes occurring quite clearly. And then you take publications like the *New York Review of Books* and the *New York Times*—they both certainly have a powerful role in creating this mainstream group. Who is in the mainstream and who is not? And of course *Esquire* comes out with its little charted thing, who is hot and who is not. So there are a lot of factors. But I believe there is a mainstream and a no-stream.

WB: Could you comment on generational shifts in African-American literature and its production?

JW: Yes, let me try if I can. Well, the newest application of a black aesthetic as I understand it is that the younger writers now represent a second generation of the black people who have been to college, and having done so and experienced things different from their parents, feel no constraint and just write about whatever it is they want to. That is well and good, but I think the old black aesthetic essentially felt the same way. The problem was that editors were not about to let you write of white love. That simply was not going to happen. Now, beyond that I am not sure what the difference is because publishing tends to keep people and groups in certain molds and channels. So we will have to see how that develops. If you wanted to talk about the progressive protest school then, of course, we have got a long tradition from the nineteenth century on. But we are now getting some postmodernist works of new structures in literature, new narrative points of view. I am not sure if that's good or bad, but I do think, in view of our inability to change the language any more than we have, that there must be something else we can do to tell the same old story. And essentially stories are the same.

WB: Would you say that what has been termed "the double consciousness" is both a burden and a gift but, above all, a great potential for a black writer in the sense that you can command more than one cultural discourse?

JW: I think it is a fantastic gift. Maybe during his time DuBois saw it as a curse. Don't forget, he was also one of the talented tenth, which made his group even smaller, more singular, so it became a curse among blacks, who thought he was too high and mighty. But I think it is an incredible gift to be able to describe not only white society but black society or any society that you are perceptive enough to understand what the hell is happening in it.

WB: I have always felt that this was one of the blessings of so-called ethnic writing as long as it is not stuck within the confines of an ethnic group, which is hard to define anyway.

JW: Well, as you know, an African-American can go to Africa, and I don't know what it is like these days, but when I first started going, around '64, in some places Africans would view you as an American even though you were black.

WB: Would you situate your work in general as an urban literature? Or as a regional literature?

JW: I have worked very hard in an unconscious way to bring the world into my small urban setting, trying to think international. *Captain Blackman* certainly is. *Jacob's Ladder* certainly is.

that doesn't happen. But I know what I'm doing, so I don't mind that much.

WB: What about language? Was that a concern of yours to use black English, colloquial levels of various strata of society?

JW: Yes, if I have to have the character to fit the language. But the more I write, the more I really do realize how limiting the language is for me. My sense was that *Beloved* had reached the point where Toni Morrison was straining to reach something else in the language, and at times this strain is quite visible.

WB: In *Jazz* it certainly is.

JW: . . . and detracting. But yes, it comes as a relief when I can deal with a character from the mean streets who is talking a language that I understand, and it can denote very simply and broadly some of the things that it would take character by character, say, at another level, three pages to do.

WB: In most of your novels your heroes, especially black men, are portrayed as marginal, beginning with your first novel, *The Angry Ones,* and its protagonist Steve Hill. Could you comment on this?

JW: Black men, generally speaking, have always been marginal.

WB: I do want to ask you about the book on Richard Pryor you did together with your son Dennis, *If I Stop I'll Die.*

JW: It is badly edited, but don't blame me. He was so much of what the people are in his language and his thoughts; he was just an incredible comedian. He did and said and thought everything every black person in the twentieth century must have said, thought, or did or wanted to do. He was just the complete comedian. Besides that, he revolutionized the whole comedy approach for whites as well. Language that was deemed unseemly became, not unlike household words, words that no longer shocked people. In terms of revolutionizing comedy and reflecting the black community and to some extent the white community, I don't think he has a peer. He is a different comedian from Bill Cosby, who is very funny in his own way.

WB: And Red Foxx, whom I like a lot.

JW: But he is brash and bold and a victim, while he victimizes people too.

WB: Into which genre would you put the book? Is it a biography? Is it a study of his art?

JW: I would call it a study because we never saw him. He just would not give us an interview. It just didn't work out. For that reason I would call it more of a study than a biography, because I think a biography has a hell of a lot of more depth. I don't think it is all that popular a book either. I think there is a lot of black history in there because we felt we had to place Pryor against the backdrop that explained his situation and the limitations that he had to perform against.

WB: In 1982 your novel *!Click Song* appeared, which, apart from being a political text, is one that deals with the topic of what it means to be a black novelist in New York. How representative a life would you say is that of Cato Caldwell Douglass? And could you briefly comment on those three "loaded" names united in one person?

JW: I hope very representative of black male writers. Cato refers to a republican (Roman). Caldwell is merely alliterative. Douglass refers to Frederick Douglass, the black abolitionist.

WB: In *!Click Song* and in *Sissie* the issues of race, beauty ideals, black family life, the relationship between black men and women play an important role. Do you see, both in "real life" and in African-American fiction, a continuum of those issues and constellations?

JW: I believe I have finished with these issues in my writing. Now it's on to gloves-off political writing on contemporary America.

SELECTED BIBLIOGRAPHY

Fernández, Roberto G. *Cuentos sin rumbo*. Miami: Ediciones Universal, 1975.
———. *La vida es un special*. Miami: Ediciones Universal, 1981.
———. *La montaña rusa*. Houston: Arte Público, 1985.
———. *Raining Backwards*. Houston: Arte Público, 1988.
———. *Holy Radishes!* Houston: Arte Público (forthcoming).
Holleran, Andrew. *Dancer from the Dance*. New York: Morrow, 1978.
———. *Nights in Aruba*. New York: Morrow, 1983.
———. *Ground Zero*. New York: NAL-Dutton, 1989.
Lelchuk, Alan. *American Mischief*. New York: Farrar, Straus & Giroux, 1973.
———. *Miriam at Thirty-Four*. 1975. New York: McGraw-Hill, 1989.
———. *Shrinking: The Beginning of My Own Ending*. Boston: Atlantic Little, Brown, 1978.
———. *Miriam in Her Forties*. 1985. New York: McGraw-Hill, 1989.
———. *On Home Ground*. New York: Harcourt, Brace, Jovanovich, 1987.
———. *Brooklyn Boy*. New York: McGraw-Hill, 1990.
———. *Playing the Game* (forthcoming).
Paley, Grace. *The Little Disturbances of Man*. 1959. New York: Viking Penguin, 1985.
———. *Enormous Changes at the Last Minute*. New York: Farrar, Straus & Giroux, 1974.
———. *Later the Same Day*. New York: Farrar, Straus & Giroux, 1985.
———. *Leaning Forward: Poems*. Penobscot, Me.: Granite Press, 1985.
———. *Long Walks and Intimate Talks*. New York: Feminist Press, 1991.
———. *New and Collected Poems*. New York: Tilbury House, 1992.
———. *The Collected Stories*. New York: Farrar, Straus & Giroux, 1994.
Reed, Ishmael. *The Free-Lance Pallbearers*. New York: Doubleday, 1967.
———. *Yellow Back Radio Broke-Down*. 1969. New York: Macmillan, 1989.
———. *Mumbo Jumbo*. 1972. New York: Macmillan, 1989.
———. *The Last Days of Louisiana Red*. 1974. New York: Macmillan, 1989.
———. *Flight to Canada*. 1976. New York: Macmillan, 1989.
———. *Shrovetide in Old New Orleans*. 1978. New York: Macmillan, 1989.
———. *The Terrible Twos*. 1982. New York: Macmillan, 1988.
———. *Reckless Eyeballing*. 1986. New York: Macmillan, 1988.

———. *Writin' Is Fightin': Thirty-Seven Years of Boxing on Paper.* 1988. New York: Macmillan, 1991.
———. *New and Collected Poems.* New York: Macmillan, 1989.
———. *The Terrible Threes.* 1989. New York: Macmillan, 1991.
———. *Airing Dirty Laundry.* Reading, Mass.: Addison-Wesley, 1993.
———. *Japanese by Spring.* New York: Macmillan, 1993.
Tapahonso, Luci. *One More Shiprock Night.* San Antonio: Tejas Art Press, 1981.
———. *Seasonal Woman.* Santa Fe, N.M.: Tooth of Time Press, 1982.
———. *A Breeze Swept Through.* Albuquerque, N.M.: West End, 1987.
———. *Sáanii Dahataał—The Women Are Singing: Poems and Stories.* Tucson, Ariz.: University of Arizona Press, 1993.
Vega, Ed. *The Comeback.* Houston: Arte Público Press, 1985.
———. *Mendoza's Dreams.* Houston: Arte Público Press, 1987.
———. *Casualty Report.* Houston: Arte Público Press, 1991.
———. *No Matter How Much You Promise to Cook or Pay the Rent You Blew it Cause Bill Bailey Ain't Never Coming Home Again.* New York: Ballantine Books, 1995.
Vizenor, Gerald. *Wordarrows: Indians and Whites in the New Fur Trade.* Minneapolis: University of Minnesota Press, 1978.
———. *Earthdivers: Tribal Narratives on Mixed Descent.* Minneapolis: University of Minnesota Press, 1981.
———. *The People Named the Chippewa: Narrative Histories.* Minneapolis: University of Minnesota Press, 1984.
———. *Griever: An American Monkey King in China.* Minneapolis: University of Minnesota Press, 1987.
———. *The Trickster of Liberty: Tribal Heirs to a Wild Baronage.* Minneapolis: University of Minnesota Press, 1988.
———. *Bearheart: The Heirship Chronicles.* Minneapolis: University of Minnesota Press, 1990 (rev. ed. of *Darkness in Saint Louis Bearheart* [Minneapolis: University of Minnesota Press, 1978]).
———. *Interior Landscapes: Autobiographical Myths and Metaphors.* Minneapolis: University of Minnesota Press, 1990.
———. *The Heirs of Columbus.* Hanover, N.H.: University Press of New England, 1991.
———. *Landfill Meditation: Crossblood Stories.* Hanover, N.H.: University Press of New England, 1991.
———. *Dead Voices: Natural Agonies in the New World.* Norman: University of Oklahoma Press, 1992.
———. *Summer in the Spring: Anishinaabe Lyric Poems and Stories.* Norman: University of Oklahoma Press, 1993.
———. *Manifest Manners.* Hanover, N.H.: University Press of New England, 1994.
———. *Shadow Distance.* Hanover, N.H.: University Press of New England, 1994.
Williams, John A. *One for New York (The Angry Ones).* New York: Ace Books, 1960.

———. *Night Song*. New York: Farrar, Straus & Giroux, 1961.
———. *Africa: Her History, Lands & People*. Savage, Md.: Cooper Square Press, 1963.
———. *Sissie*. New York: Farrar, Straus & Giroux, 1963.
———. *The Protectors*. New York: Farrar, Straus & Giroux, 1964.
———. *This Is My Country Too*. New York: NAL/World, 1965.
———. *The Man Who Cried I Am*. Boston: Little, Brown, 1967.
———. *Sons of Darkness, Sons of Light*. Boston: Little, Brown, 1969.
———. *The King God Didn't Save: Martin Luther King, Jr.* New York: Coward McCann, 1970.
———. *The Most Native Sons: Richard Wright*. New York: Doubleday, 1970.
———. *Captain Blackman*. New York: Doubleday, 1972.
———. *Flashbacks: A Twenty-Year Diary of Article Writing*. New York: Doubleday, 1973.
———. *Minorities in the City*. New York: Harper & Row, 1975.
———. *Mothersill and the Foxes*. New York: Doubleday, 1975.
———. *The Junior Bachelor Society*. New York: Doubleday, 1976.
———. *!Click Song*. Boston: Houghton Mifflin, 1982.
———. *The Berhama Account*. Far Hills, N.J.: New Horizon Press, 1985.
———. *Jacob's Ladder*. New York: Thunder's Mouth Press, 1987.
Williams, John A., and Dennis A. Williams. *If I Stop I'll Die: The Comedy and Tragedy of Richard Pryor*. New York: Thunder's Mouth Press, 1991.

UNIVERSITY PRESS OF NEW ENGLAND publishes books under its own imprint and is the publisher for Brandeis University Press, Brown University Press, Dartmouth College, Middlebury College Press, University of New Hampshire, University of Rhode Island, Tufts University, University of Vermont, Wesleyan University Press, and Salzburg Seminar.

ABOUT THE EDITORS

Helmbrecht Breinig and Wolfgang Binder are professors of American Studies (Amerikanistik) at the University of Erlangen-Nürnberg. Breinig is author of Satire und Roman: Studien zur Theorie des Genrekonflikts und zur satirischen Erzählliteratur der USA von Brackenridge bis Vonnegut*; Binder is author of* Europäisches Drama und amerikanische Kritik: Skandinavische, deutschsprachige und russische Dramatiker in der nordamerikanischen Kritik, 1890–1914.

Library of Congress Cataloging-in-Publication Data

American contradictions : interviews on culture and writing / edited by Wolfgang Binder and Helmbrecht Breinig.

p. cm.

Originally published in German. The interviews contained in this volume were together with a selection of literary texts as "Facing America: Multikulturelle Literatur der heutigen U.S.A. in Texten und Interviews, ein Lesebuch", by Rotpunktverlag Zurich, 1994.

ISBN 0-8195-5282-8. — ISBN 0-8195-6288-2 (pbk.)

1. American literature—Minority authors—History and criticism—Theory, etc. 2. United States—Literatures—History and criticism—Theory, etc. 3. Authors, American—20th century—Interviews. 4. Pluralism (Social sciences) in literature. 5. Language and culture—United States. 6. Ethnic groups in literature. 7. Minorities in literature. I. Binder, Wolfgang. II. Breinig, Helmbrecht.

PS153.M56A4 1995

810.9'920693—dc20 94-39055

∞